First World War
and Army of Occupation
War Diary
France, Belgium and Germany

42 DIVISION
Headquarters, Branches and Services
Royal Army Ordnance Corps
Deputy Assistant Director Ordnance Services
1 March 1917 - 28 February 1919

WO95/2648/3

The Naval & Military Press Ltd
www.nmarchive.com
Published in association with The National Archives

Published by

The Naval & Military Press Ltd

Unit 10 Ridgewood Industrial Park,

Uckfield, East Sussex,

TN22 5QE England

Tel: +44 (0) 1825 749494

www.naval-military-press.com

www.nmarchive.com

This diary has been reprinted in facsimile from the original. Any imperfections are inevitably reproduced and the quality may fall short of modern type and cartographic standards.

© Crown Copyright
Images reproduced by permission of The National Archives, London, England, 2015.

Contents

Document type	Place/Title	Date From	Date To
Heading	WO95/2648/3		
Heading	42nd Division Dep. Asst Dir. Ordnance Serv. 1917 Mar Feb 1919		
Heading	War Diary Of D.A.D.O.S. 42nd Division from 1st March 1917 to 31st March 1917 Vol II		
War Diary	Pont Remy	01/03/1917	31/03/1917
Heading	War Diary of D.A.D.O.S. 42nd Division from 1st May to 31st May 1917 Vol I		
Miscellaneous	Central Registry Subject And Office Of Origin		
War Diary	Doingt	01/05/1917	01/05/1917
War Diary	Roisel	03/05/1917	20/05/1917
War Diary	Rocquigny	21/05/1917	31/05/1917
Heading	War Diary of D.A.D.O.S. 42nd Division from 1st June 1917 to 1st July 1917 Volume I		
War Diary	Rocquigny	01/06/1917	28/06/1917
Heading	War Diary of D.A.D.O.S. 42nd Division from 1st July 1917 to 31st July 1917 Volume VII		
War Diary	Rocquigny	01/07/1917	08/07/1917
War Diary	Achiet Le Grand	09/07/1917	30/07/1917
Heading	War Diary of D.A.D.O.S. 42nd Division from 1st August 1917 to 31st August 1917		
War Diary	Achiet-Le Grand	01/08/1917	22/08/1917
War Diary	Poperinghe	23/08/1917	31/08/1917
Heading	War Diary of D.A.D.O.S. 42nd Division from 1st September 1917 to 30th September 1917		
War Diary	H.7.d. 5.9 Sheet 28	01/09/1917	17/09/1917
War Diary	Watou	18/09/1917	22/09/1917
War Diary	Rosendael	23/09/1917	23/09/1917
War Diary	St Idesbald	24/09/1917	30/09/1917
Heading	War Diary Of D.A.D.O.S. 42nd Division October 1st to 31st 1917		
War Diary	St Idesbald (Furnes Map W. 10 B 3.6)	01/10/1917	07/10/1917
War Diary	Coxyde Bains	10/10/1917	31/10/1917
Heading	War Diary of D.A.D.O.S. 42nd Division November 1917		
War Diary	Coxyde Bains	01/11/1917	18/11/1917
War Diary	Aire-Sur-La-Lys	19/11/1917	28/11/1917
War Diary	Locon	29/11/1917	30/11/1917
Heading	War Diary of D.A.D.O.S. 42nd Division December 1917		
War Diary	Locon	01/12/1917	31/12/1917
Heading	War Diary January 1918 D.A.D.O.S. 42nd Division.		
War Diary	Locon	02/01/1918	30/01/1918
Heading	War Diary D.A.D.O.S. 42nd Div. February 1918		
War Diary	Locon	01/02/1918	10/02/1918
War Diary	Busnes	13/02/1918	28/02/1918
Heading	War Diary March 1918 D.A.D.O.S. 42nd Division		
War Diary	Busnes	01/03/1918	03/03/1918
War Diary	Lafencrece	04/03/1918	22/03/1918
War Diary	Basseux	23/03/1918	25/03/1918

War Diary	St Amand	26/03/1918	29/03/1918
War Diary	Beanrepaire	30/03/1918	31/03/1918
Heading	War Diary D.A.D.O.S. 42nd Division April 1918 Vol 15		
War Diary	Beanrepaire	03/04/1918	06/04/1918
War Diary	Pas	07/04/1918	15/04/1918
War Diary	Coven	16/04/1918	30/04/1918
Heading	War Diary of D.A.D.O.S. 42nd Division May 1918 Vol 16		
War Diary	Couth	03/05/1918	04/05/1918
War Diary	Pas	05/05/1918	31/05/1918
Heading	War Diary of D.A.D.O.S. 42nd Division June 1918 Vol 17		
War Diary	Pas-En-Artois	02/06/1918	28/06/1918
Heading	War Diary of D.A.D.O.S. 42nd Division July 1918 Vol 18		
War Diary	Bus-les-Artois	01/07/1918	08/07/1918
War Diary	Sarton	09/07/1918	16/07/1918
War Diary	Authie	18/07/1918	31/07/1918
Heading	War Diary of D.A.D.O.S. 42nd Division Vol 19		
War Diary	Authie	03/08/1918	15/08/1918
War Diary	Bus-les-Artois	16/08/1918	29/08/1918
War Diary	Merament	30/08/1918	30/08/1918
War Diary	Pys	31/08/1918	31/08/1918
Heading	War Diary September 1918 D.A.D.O.S. 42nd Divn Vol 20		
War Diary	Pys	02/09/1918	21/09/1918
War Diary	Lebucquiere	22/09/1918	29/09/1918
Heading	War Diary October 1918 D.A.D.O.S. 42nd Division		
War Diary	Ruyaulcourt	02/10/1918	09/10/1918
War Diary	Esnes	10/10/1918	13/10/1918
War Diary	Beauvois	14/10/1918	31/10/1918
Heading	War Diary November D.A.D.O.S. 42nd Division		
War Diary	Beauvois	01/11/1918	05/11/1918
War Diary	Le Quesnoy	06/11/1918	10/11/1918
War Diary	Maison Rouge	11/11/1918	14/11/1918
War Diary	Hautmont	15/11/1918	29/11/1918
Heading	War Diary of D.A.D.O.S. 42nd Division December 1918 Vol 23		
War Diary	Hautmont	02/12/1918	13/12/1918
War Diary	Charleroi	14/12/1918	24/12/1918
Heading	War Diary for the month of January 1919 D.A.D.O.S. 42nd Division		
War Diary	Charleroi	07/01/1919	30/01/1919
Heading	War Diary for the month of February 1919 D.A.D.O.S. 42nd Division		
War Diary	Charleroi	01/02/1919	01/02/1919
War Diary	Belgium	02/02/1919	28/02/1919

WO 95
2648/3

42ND DIVISION

DEP. ASST DIR. ORDNANCE SERV.

1917 MAR ~~MAY 1917~~ - FEB 1919

(APR 1917 MISSING)

Confidential

War Diary — Vol 2

of

D.A.D.O.S., 42nd Division

from 1st March 1917 to 31st March 1917

Vol. II.

Army Form C. 2118.

WAR DIARY
INTELLIGENCE SUMMARY.
(Erase heading not required.)

Instructions regarding War Diaries and Intelligence Summaries are contained in F. S. Regs., Part II. and the Staff Manual respectively. Title pages will be prepared in manuscript.

Place	Date	Hour	Summary of Events and Information	Remarks and references to Appendices
Port Remy	1/3/17		Arrived at Port Remy with Advance Party to await Division.	
	2/3/17		Visited C.O.O., Abbeville & drew Camp Kettles for use of parties detraining + arranged for issue of Waistcoats Cardigan	
	3/3/17	5 p.m.	125th Infantry Brigade detraining — Sub-Condr. Hardy, A.O.C. + 2 Other ranks arrived. Temporary stores Hoppies opened in Cycle Shop.	
	4/3/17		4 Lorries with drivers received from Advance M.T. Depot sent to Abbeville to draw part of rifles received from Base for re-arming Division	
	5/3/17	7 a.m.	D.H.Q. + part 126 Infantry Brigade arrived. Advance personnel D.H.Q. remaining at Port Remy with M.T. instead of proceeding to Hallencourt.	
	6/3/17		Registers & Records for B.E.F. commenced. Arrangements made with Staff Captain 125 Infantry Brigade for Battalions to parade by Companies at intervals of one hour and draw rifles, bayonets, full through steel helmets. Lorries employed in bringing consignments sent by Base, from Replenishing Station, Abbeville, to Port Remy.	
	7/3/17		Battalions of 125 Infantry Bde. commencing with 5th Lancashire Fusiliers issued with short rifles, bayonets pattern 1907, steel helmets, and Anti-Gas equipment.	
	8/3/17		ditto	

Army Form C. 2118.

WAR DIARY
INTELLIGENCE SUMMARY.
(Erase heading not required.)

Instructions regarding War Diaries and Intelligence Summaries are contained in F. S. Regs., Part II. and the Staff Manual respectively. Title pages will be prepared in manuscript.

Place	Date	Hour	Summary of Events and Information	Remarks and references to Appendices
Fort Henry	9/3/17		Equipping 125 Infantry Brigade with Rifles & Steel Helmets.	
do	10/3/17		ditto	
Fort Henry	11/3/17	9am	To Villers-Bretonneux to interview A.D.O.S. III Corps by car.	
		7pm	127 Infantry Brigade detrained & Ordnance personnel of Brigade H.Q. joined me.	
do	11/3/17		127 Infantry Brigade issued by Battalions with short rifles, bayonets, steel helmets & Anti gas equipment.	
	12/3/17	all	ditto.	
	13/3/17	day	ditto	
	14/3/17		ditto.	
	15/3/17		To Advanced Horse Transport Depot by car to arrange about vehicles & harness to be drawn by Divisions.	
	16/3/17		Extra billet taken up as office & house of Mlle Allard, Fort Henry.	

Army Form C. 2118.

WAR DIARY
INTELLIGENCE SUMMARY.
(Erase heading not required.)

Instructions regarding War Diaries and Intelligence Summaries are contained in F. S. Regs., Part II. and the Staff Manual respectively. Title pages will be prepared in manuscript.

Place	Date	Hour	Summary of Events and Information	Remarks and references to Appendices
Pont Remy	17/3/17	10 am	To Abbeville by car. Interviewed C.O. Interviewed C.O. arranges that artillery units of Division, who were quartered in Carus area, should find rifles. Quote Hernute &c at Esteville to save extra journey to Pont Remy.	
	18/3/17		Final units of 126 Infantry Brigade drawing Antigas equipment Steel Helmets &c. This Brigade having lost arrived	
	19/3/17		ditto	
	20/3/17		Divisional units completed with shot or E.Y. rifles, Bayonets Steel Helmets & Anti-Gas Equipment. Issue of field service boots proceeding – one pair ankle boots being returned.	
	21/3/17		Lorries with Brigade W.O. sent to Hamel to convey shoes to 125 Infantry Brigade who has moved up.	
	22/3/17		To Div. H.Q. by car to interview A.A. & Q.M.G. with reference to formation of Divisional Baths & provision of initial stock of clothing	
	23/3/17		Ordnance personnel 125 Inf Bde sent to Cappy to take up quarters	

Army Form C. 2118.

D.A.D.O.S.
42 Division.
4th Sheet. March 1917

WAR DIARY
INTELLIGENCE SUMMARY.
(Erase heading not required.)

Place	Date	Hour	Summary of Events and Information	Remarks and references to Appendices
Pont Remy	24/3/17		To Villers-Bretonneux by car to interview A.D.O.S. III Corps	
	25/3/17		To Calloy; saw Town Major & Ordnance W.O. 125 Infantry Brigade & to office of A.D.O.S. III Corps to attend weekly conference of D.A.D'sO.S.	
	26/3/17		D.R.O. by car to interview "Q" on various matters. Artillery training with 18 pdrs, 18/m Q.F. Ordnance.	
	27/3/17		To COD Abbeville & R.A. Headquarters in connection with new 18/m Q.F. Ordnance issues to 42 Division.	
	28/3/17		Ordnance W.O. of new 127 Infantry Brigade Headquarters out to Calloy to take up quarters in previously Battalion of 127 Infantry Brigade.	
	29/3/17		To Calloy by car. Gave various instructions to Brigade Warrant Officers, 125 & 127 Infantry Brigades.	
	30/3/17		Service despatches to 3 Infantry Brigades	
	31/3/17		To Abbeville. Interviewed C.O.O. re return of surpluses & interviewed O.C. Aux. Horse Transport Depot & D.O.S. of 8th9 I.G.C.	

G.M.Summers Capt
a/D.A.D.O.S. 42 Divn

Confidential

Vol 4

War Diary

of

D.A.D.O.S., 42nd Division

From 1st May to 31st May 1917

(Volume 1)

Army Form A. 2007.

CENTRAL REGISTRY.

Central Registry No. and Date.

Attached Files.

SUBJECT, AND OFFICE OF ORIGIN.

Referred to	Date.	Referred to	Date.	Referred to	Date.
				P. A.	Date.

Schedule of Correspondence.

WAR DIARY
INTELLIGENCE SUMMARY

Army Form C. 2118.

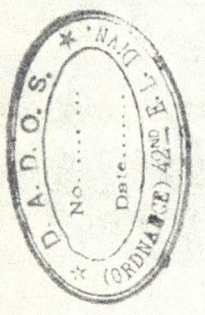

Place	Date	Hour	Summary of Events and Information	Remarks and references to Appendices
Doingt	1/5/17		A.D.O.S. visited Roisel and arranged site for Ordnance dump at K11 c.2.5. Sheet 62c.	A.1.S.
Roisel	3/5/17		Store dump to move to site near Roisel. Capt Potter (D.D.O.S.) resumed duties & took over control from Capt G.G.B. Bannerman (A)DADOS	A.1.S.
	4/5/17		DADOS visited Railhead, Scrouve, & arranged return of unserviceable stores	A.1.S.
	5/5/17		DADOS visited various units with regard to disposal of Tents with Cutch. Conferred with Staff Captain, 126 Brigade.	A.1.S.
	6/5/17		To III Corps Workshops Scrouve to see Sgm. & arrange fitting of Motor Haulage at the burn to 14 ton Wagons.	A.1.S.
	8/5/17		Railhead opened at Roisel. Ordnance stores to be detrained there. "M.I." refers to A.D.O.S. III Corps of recommendations for advancement in Corps Pay.	A.1.S.
	9/5/17		Return of all Clothing issued to Division during March & April furnished to A.D.O.S. III Corps.	A.1.S.

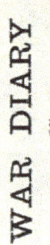

WAR DIARY
INTELLIGENCE SUMMARY
(Erase heading not required.)

Army Form C. 2118.

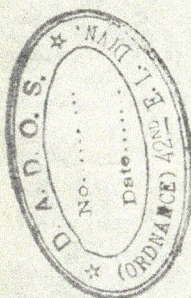

Place	Date	Hour	Summary of Events and Information	Remarks and references to Appendices
	11/3/17		Visited Peronne & arranged storage of returned Winter Clothing in French Barracks.	Fr. 9
	12/3/17		To Peronne. Arranged loading of Trucks for Winter Clothing with R.T.O. Two L.O.M. Corps workshops also running Motor Wagons	Fr. 9
	14/3/17		Loaded 18 hr gun carriages to replace one of 210 Bell. R.F.A. damaged by (erased) Were reported to Army H.Q. &c. Also wires for Lewis guns complete for Workshops Dept.	Fr. 9
	16/3/17		Winter Clothing in course of loading up at Peronne. One lorry, 1 Act. N.C.O. & 2 lorry men detailed for duty at Peronne under Officer A.O.D. approved by Corps to take charge of one lorry from each Division for return of winter clothing to Motors to be enquiry to D.A.D.O.S. 20th Division with a view to taking over his a/c.	Fr. 9
	17/3/17			Fr. 9

Army Form C. 2118.

WAR DIARY
or
INTELLIGENCE SUMMARY.
(Erase heading not required.)

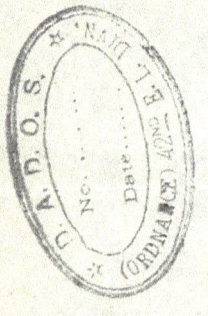

Place	Date	Hour	Summary of Events and Information	Remarks and references to Appendices
Roisel	18/5/17		Held Board of Survey on unserviceable Winter Clothing returned by Division	F.9
	20/5/17		Visited Army Headquarters & consulted D.D.O.S. II Army referened return of S.D. clothing. Interviewed A.D.O.S. XV Corps	F.9
Roquigny	22/5/17		Moved dump/personnel & effects to Roquigny - started 5% 0.27 a.8.8.	F.9
	23/5/17		Reception sheds for unserviceable clothing to opened. Class "B" men employed for sorting and packing purposes	F.9
	24/5/17		A.D.O.S. XV Corps inspected stores &c. Conferred with him on scheme to Bases for guns &c.	F.9
	25/5/17		To Amiens by car for purchase of amulets to respirators by Division	F.9
	26/5/17		Detachment inspected and drilled by Gas Officer.	F.9

Army Form C. 2118.

WAR DIARY
INTELLIGENCE SUMMARY.
(Erase heading not required.)

Instructions regarding War Diaries and Intelligence Summaries are contained in F. S. Regs., Part II. and the Staff Manual respectively. Title pages will be prepared in manuscript.

D.A.D.O.S. ORDNANCE 42ND E.L. DIVN.

Place	Date	Hour	Summary of Events and Information	Remarks and references to Appendices
Rocquigny	27/5/17		A/A + QMG inspected dump + clothing return sheds. Discussed with him issues of underclothing through Baths + Laundry etc.	F.9
	29/5/17		Went to A.D.O.S. XV Corps by car + discussed his list of Returns required + French lorries taken over by Division	F.9
	30/5/17		Visited Wagon lines of units and inspected vehicles. Nearly all badly in need of paint. Wrote to base hastening arrival of Division had not had any service paint since arrival in France.	F.9
	31/5/17		Visited Divisional Headquarters + saw A.A + Q.M.G. Informed him, base had no service colour paint available the promises to obtain approval of G.O.C. to local Purchase.	F.9

F.L. Potter
Captain
D.A.D.O.S. 42nd Division

Vol 5

Confidential

War Diary

of

D.A.D.O.S., 42nd Division

from 1st June 1917 to 1st July 1917.

(Volume 1)

WAR DIARY
INTELLIGENCE SUMMARY.
(Erase heading not required.)

Army Form C. 2118.

Instructions regarding War Diaries and Intelligence Summaries are contained in F. S. Regs., Part II. and the Staff Manual respectively. Title pages will be prepared in manuscript.

Place	Date	Hour	Summary of Events and Information	Remarks and references to Appendices
Acquigny	1/6/17		Called on A.D.O.S. III Corps and arranged with him that I.O.M. should examine 18-pr gun with "A" Battery 210 Brigade R.F.A. Went to O.O., IV Army Troops by car & brought back Extractors for Stokes 3 in Mortars	F.9.
do	2/6/17		Division re-transferred 6 III Corps	F.9.
do	5/6/17		Armourers shop established with 8 Armourers in Wheatown from Bus. Engaged on fixing steel visors	F.9.
do	7/6/17		All clothes dump commenced for Service Dress and all kinds of boots. Clothes shed commenced for reception of unserviceable equipment.	F.9.
do	8/6/17		"Yukon" packs issues to Division for trial	F.9.
do	9/6/17		D.A.D.O.S. went to Amiens to purchase White Paint and Fly traps	F.9.

WAR DIARY
or
INTELLIGENCE SUMMARY.

Army Form C. 2118.

Place	Date	Hour	Summary of Events and Information	Remarks and references to Appendices
Becquigny	10/6/17	11am	D.A.D.O.S went to Ethicourt to Corps Headquarters to attend conference of D.A.D.s O.S.	F.J.9
do	16/6/17	11am	D.D.O.S. Fourth Army & A.D.O.S. III Corps called round. Inspected Armourers and Bootmakers shop, Old Clothes Store & Stores generally	F.J.
do	17/6/17	11am	Attended conference of D.A.D.s O.S. at III Corps Hqrs at Ethicourt	F.J.9
do	18/6/17		Went to 3rd Corps Laundry at Bray with A.D.O.S. to see how it was being run.	F.J.9
do	19/6/17		Bootmakers Shop established at my Camp with 5 shoemakers	F.J.9
do	20/6/17		Went to Amiens to purchase stencils, Paint, Brushes, Scythes for Haymakers &c.	F.J.9

Army Form C. 2118.

WAR DIARY
or
INTELLIGENCE SUMMARY.
(Erase heading not required.)

Instructions regarding War Diaries and Intelligence Summaries are contained in F. S. Regs., Part II. and the Staff Manual respectively. Title pages will be prepared in manuscript.

Place	Date	Hour	Summary of Events and Information	Remarks and references to Appendices
Hazebrouck	21/6/17		Hot food containers received new from Base, issued to Division.	879
do	23/6/17		Visited No. 20 Workshop with reference to fitting attachments for Motor Haulage to Pontoon Wagons.	879
do	24/6/17		Ten Incidero Shop commenced.	879
do	28/6/17		Visited Haymakers Park No. 2 and arranged for issue of Oil, Soap etc.	879

J. T. Potter
Captain
D.A.D.O.S. 42nd Division

Confidential.

War Diary

of
D.A.D.O.S. 42nd Division

From 1st July 1917 to 31st July 1917.

Volume VII

Vol 6

Army Form C. 2118.

WAR DIARY
or
INTELLIGENCE SUMMARY.
(Erase heading not required.)

July 1917

Place	Date	Hour	Summary of Events and Information	Remarks and references to Appendices
Roquigny	1/7/17		Armourer Staff Sergeant sent from Divisional Shop to inspect rifles of 1/5 Lancashire Fusiliers. Rifles received 500. Dirty barrels 85. Other defects 135. Copy of his report in full sent to O.C. Battalion and to Headquarters 125 Infantry Brigade	J.S.
	2/7/17	10 a.m.	D.A.D.O.S. went to Achiet-le-Grand & arranged for occupation of site now held by Ordnance, 58th Division to be taken over on 9th inst.	J.S.
	3/7/17		Two Armourer Staff Sergeants sent from Divisional Shop to inspect rifles & Lewis Machine guns of 1/5 Lancs. Fusiliers. Engaged all day.	J.S.
	4/7/17		Inspection of rifles &c of 1/6 Lancs. Fus. completed. Report received by Armourer forwarded to O.C. Battn. & Staff Captain, 125 Infantry Brigade. D.A.D.O.S. to Amiens by car to purchase material for binding & thatching to required by Divisional Haymaking Party	J.S.
	5/7/17		Reports received from Brase that a German Machine Gun has been returned here as salved. No. &c of M.G. issued to Division for instructional purposes. Apparently lost by Machine Gun Corps in previous D.HQ. informed.	J.S.

Army Form C. 2118.

WAR DIARY
or
INTELLIGENCE SUMMARY.
(Erase heading not required.)

July.

Instructions regarding War Diaries and Intelligence Summaries are contained in F. S. Regs., Part II. and the Staff Manual respectively. Title pages will be prepared in manuscript.

Place	Date	Hour	Summary of Events and Information	Remarks and references to Appendices
Gorguigny	6/7/17		Armourers report on Lewis guns & rifles of 1/8th Lancs Fusiliers forwarded to Staff Captain, 125 Infantry Brigade with request for report as to action taken in respect of apparent neglect.	G.9.
do	do		D.A.D.O.S. 58th Division with two Brigade Warrant Officers called, inspected dump preparatory to taking it over from us, & promised to leave two store tents standing at Achiet-le-Grand to be occupied by my stores and staff. A general exchange of accommodation was arranged as far as possible.	F.T.9.
do	7/7/17		Instructions received that III Corps now administered by Third Army.	
do	8/7/17		D.A.D.O.S. visited new site at Achiet-le-Grand. A.D.O.S. & D.A.D.O.S. informed that Divisional Artillery left behind to be administered by 57th Division	
Achiet-le-Grand	9/7/17		D.A.D.O.S. & personnel, Armourers Shop moved by lorry to Achiet-le-Grand & took over site previously occupied by D.A.D.O.S. 58th Division at Sheet 57c F.T.9. G.9.b.7.4. Division absorbed in VI Corps.	
do	10/7/17		G.O.C., 42nd Division (Maj. Gen. the Hon. B.P. Mitford) inspected stores & accommodation of Ord Ordnance, and directed that a copy of every report rendered by an Armourer after inspection of any unit's machine guns or rifles should be furnished him as soon as possible after the inspection.	G.9.
do	11/7/17		D.A.D.O.S. visited Ribemont and interviewed A.D.O.S. VI Corps. D.D.O.S. III Army inspected stores & Armourers Shop.	F.T.9.

Army Form C. 2118.

WAR DIARY
or
INTELLIGENCE SUMMARY.
(Erase heading not required.)

Instructions regarding War Diaries and Intelligence Summaries are contained in F. S. Regs., Part II. and the Staff Manual respectively. Title pages will be prepared in manuscript.

Place	Date	Hour	Summary of Events and Information	Remarks and references to Appendices
Achiet le Grand	12/6/17	9am	Two Armourer Staff Sergeants sent to examine rifles and Lewis Machine guns of 1/8th Lancashire Fusiliers	379
"	"	3pm	8 Vickers Machine Guns of 125 M.G. Coy received in Divisional Armourers Shop for overhaul.	379
"	"		D.A.D.O.S. motored to Third Army Gun Park to ascertain what stores were held there; and also to Heavy Mobile Workshop to make arrangements for reception of M/S wheels &c.	379
	13/6/17		New pattern slings for firing Lewis guns from the hip received from Base, and issued, one to each Infantry Brigade for trial. Brigades to report to D.H.Q. result of trials	379
	14/6/17		D.A.D.O.S. went to Corps Headquarters. Interviewed A.D.O.S. re Corps reference to replacements of personnel and generally.	379
	15/6/17		D.A.D.O.S. attended conference of D.A.D.O.S. at Corps Headquarters	379
	17/6/17		D.A.D.O.S. visited Staff Captain 126 Infantry Brigade to arrange inspection of all rifles and Machine Guns	379

WAR DIARY
or
INTELLIGENCE SUMMARY.
(Erase heading not required.)

Army Form C. 2118.

Place	Date	Hour	Summary of Events and Information	Remarks and references to Appendices
Asfield to Grand	18/6/17		Assembly of Conference at Corps Headquarters D.A.D.O.S. of VII & 62nd Divisions shown over Armourer's Shop and explained of working explained.	J.T.9.
	20/6/17		A.A. & Q.M.G. 42nd Division inspected stores and camp.	J.T.9.
	21/6/17		D.A.D.O.S. visited Gun Park with reference to 3 Lewis Guns for instructional purposes required by Division	J.T.9.
	23/6/17		D.A.D.O.S. visited Staff Captain 126 Infantry Brigade with reference to amounts of clothing issued to Brigade as compared with serviceable returns. Visited 428 Field Coy. & 10th Manchester Regt.	J.T.9.
	24/6/17		Armourers carried out inspection of rifles and machine guns of 126th & 127th Infantry Brigades. Two Armourers sent from shops to assist the two Armourers in each Brigade to fit work his unit.	J.T.9.
	4/9/17		Written report of Armourers collected on completion of inspection	J.T.9.

WAR DIARY
or
INTELLIGENCE SUMMARY.

Army Form C. 2118.

July

Place	Date	Hour	Summary of Events and Information	Remarks and references to Appendices
Achiet le Grand	30/7/17		Copies of Armourers' Reports sent to A.D.V.S. M.G. and also to respective Brigade Headquarters for necessary action.	9/3.

Murgatroyd
Major for O/C MGS
42. Divn.

Confidential

Vol 7

War Diary
of
D.A.D.O.S. 42nd Division

From: 1st August 1917.
To: 31st August 1917.

D.A.D.O.S.
42ND
(E.L.) DIVISION.
2.9.17

Army Form C. 2118.

WAR DIARY
INTELLIGENCE SUMMARY. August 1917.
(Erase heading not required.)

Place	Date	Hour	Summary of Events and Information	Remarks and references to Appendices
Achiet-le-Grand	1/8/17	2pm	D.O.S., B.E.F. accompanied by D.D.O.S., Third Army and A.D.O.S., VI Corps inspected store arrangements, Armourers Shop and lines	A.19
do	2/8/17		Three Chaff Cutters drawn from III Corps Troops for issue to 3 Infantry Brigades	A.19
do	3/8/17		Lorries sent to Third Army Gun Park and Heavy Mobile Workshops for Lewis gun parts, binoculars & wheels.	A.13
do	4/8/17		D.A.D.O.S. visited Amiens by car for purchase of sewing machines, soldering irons, fluid gum arabic for pasting targets.	A.13
do	9/8/17		D.A.Q.M.G., 42nd Divn (vice D.A.D.O.S. on leave) with Warrant Officer went to Amiens to purchase sewing machines looked out by D.A.D.O.S. on 4/8/17.	A.13
do	11/8/17		3 Sewing Machines brought from Amiens by lorry.	A.13

WAR DIARY
INTELLIGENCE SUMMARY
August 1917

Army Form C. 2118.

Place	Date	Hour	Summary of Events and Information	Remarks and references to Appendices
Achiet le Grand	12/8/17		Maj. General B. Mitford. C.B. G.O.C. 42nd Division inspected Ordnance stores workshops of D.A.D.O.S.	S.9.
do	17/8/17		50 ser E.L. Sackenddery drawn from D.A.D.O.S. 50th Division	S.9.
do	18/8/17		D.A.D.O.S. (Capt. J. Potter) resumed duties of D.A.D.O.S. on return from leave	S.9.
do	21/8/17		Two truckloads of stores railed to new area to which Division would move.	S.9.
do	22/8/17		Stores and personnel moved to Poperinghe by lorry and chung established at Place Bertin No 18.	S.9.
Poperinghe	23/8/17		D.A.D.O.S. visited new Railhead, and A.D.O.S. XIX Corps. Return of personnel & Divisional Order of Battle furnished to A.D.O.S.	S.9.
	25/8/17		Outstanding demands from Artillery units received from D.A.D.O.S. 9th Division. Artillery entraining to rejoin 42nd Division. Skeleton cases for carrying water two received.	S.9.

Army Form C. 2118.

WAR DIARY
INTELLIGENCE SUMMARY.
(Erase heading not required.)

August 1917

Place	Date	Hour	Summary of Events and Information	Remarks and references to Appendices
Spinghk	26/8/17		Stores continued to demands transferred from Havre Base to Calais Base received and distributed.	373.
do	27/8/17		A.D.O.S. XIX Corps called. Piccadilly E.D. received to Artillery and other units.	373.
do	28/8/17		Divisional Artillery relieved Artillery in line. D.A.D.O.S. saw Staff Captain R.A. to ensure all spares taken from guns before exchange with outgoing Batteries.	373.
do	29/8/17		D.A.D.O.S. visited quarters of D.A.D.O.S. 15th Division with a view to taking over his dumps; and visited D.H.Q. spr. 10 & 56 Light Workshops. D.A.D.O.S. called on A.D.O.S. XIX Corps	373.
do	30/8/17		D.A.D.O.S. called on Staff Captain 124 Infantry Brigade and I.O.M. Light Ordnance Workshops.	373.
do	31/8/17		D.D.O.S. Personnel moved to site at H.9.d.5.9 sheet 28 & established stores & shops	373.

Confidential

Vol 7 & 8

War Diary
of
D.A.D.O.S. 42nd Division
from
1st September 1917
to
30th September 1917.

Army Form C. 2118

WAR DIARY

INTELLIGENCE SUMMARY

(Erase heading not required.)

September 1917

Place	Date	Hour	Summary of Events and Information	Remarks and references to Appendices
September 1 H.q.5.9 Sheet 28	1/9/17		DADOS visited DDOS V Army by car re return to Woolwich of Army QM Sergt Neal AOC. - Tube expired; and asked for replacement, further issue of Horse Respirators in the Division, but was informed no more available.	F9
do	3/9/17		38th Army Bde RFA attached to Division for Ordnance administration. 1 Sewing Machine purchased for 1/6 Lancashire Fusiliers by DADOS in D Omer.	F9
do	5/9/17		DADOS took Clinometers for repair by car to Heavy Mobile Workshops & brought Field Dressings for Infantry + Black Watch from 1/2 E Lancs Field Ambulance. Attended at office of ADOS XIX Corps.	F9
do	6/9/17		59th Divisional Artillery attached to Division. 1 Sergeant + 1 storeman joined from DADOS. 59th Divn to administer under DADOS 42nd Divn.	F9
do	7/9/17		5th Aus " Divl Arty transferred to 1st Anzac Corps Troops. V Corps relieved XIX.	F9
do	8/9/17		64th, 86th & 238th Army Bdes RFA attached to 42nd Divn for Ordnance administration.	F9

Army Form C. 2118.

Sheet 2

WAR DIARY
or
INTELLIGENCE SUMMARY.
(Erase heading not required.)

Instructions regarding War Diaries and Intelligence Summaries are contained in F. S. Regs., Part II. and the Staff Manual respectively. Title pages will be prepared in manuscript.

Place	Date	Hour	Summary of Events and Information	Remarks and references to Appendices
Hq d. 59. Sheet 28	14/9/17	2 pm	A.D.O.S. V Corps inspected stores dump & clerical system.	79
	15/9/17		D.A.D.O.S. visited D.S.O. 42 Div & Staff Captain, 127th Infantry Brigade.	79
	16/9/17	7 pm	Store tents & compound shelled by enemy guns. One store tent slightly damaged & one or two boxes of soap stolen. No casualties. Seven or eight rounds, apparently about 15cm calibre. Shell holes filled in. All artillery transferred to 9th Division.	79
	17/9/17	7 pm	Ordnance dump & personnel moved by lorry to Watou.	79
Watou	18/9/17		D.A.D.O.S. visited D.A.D.O.S. 9th Division with reference to transfer of Corps Area stores.	79
	19/9/17		D.A.D.O.S. visited Poperinghe to attend D.H.Q, & called on Railhead Ordnance Officer.	79
	20/9/17		do	79
	21/9/17		Orders received to move to Coyde.	& on Divn. Light Workshops 79

WAR DIARY or INTELLIGENCE SUMMARY

Army Form C. 2118.
Sheet 3
September 1917

Place	Date	Hour	Summary of Events and Information	Remarks and references to Appendices
Watou	22/9/17	8 am	DADOS & Chief Clerk proceeded by car to La Panne. Ordnance personnel sent as ferry lorry to Rousdaal (Dunkerque). DADOS reported to ADOS XV Corps at Bray Dunes.	
Rousdaal	23/9/17		DADOS visited ADOS 32nd Divn with a view to taking over his site at Coxyde Bains. Personnel moved to St Idesbald with Ordnance 66th Division.	
St Ides bald	24/9/17		Office dump taken over from DADOS 66th Division. Lights, Anti-Aircraft & Mountings for Lewis guns drawn from OC Corps Troops.	
do.	26/9/17		DADOS visited DDOS Fourth Army reference Category "A" personnel; and also Divisional Supply Column at Millo-les-Bains.	
do.	28/9/17		Armourers sent from shop for duty at Corps Lewis Gun School	
do.	29/9/17		DADOS with DAQMG visited Dep.31 Battalion at Corps Reinforcement Camp & Heavy Mobile Workshops.	
do.	30/9/17		DADOS visited Staff Captain 127th Infantry Brigade reference return of bicycles & went to Poielend Ordnance 32 Divn.	

3

Vol 9

42.

War Diary.
of
D.A.D.O.S. 42nd Division

October 1st to 31st 1914.

Army Form C. 2118.

Sheet 1

WAR DIARY
—of—
INTELLIGENCE SUMMARY
(Erase heading not required.)

October 1917

Instructions regarding War Diaries and Intelligence Summaries are contained in F.S. Regs., Part II. and the Staff Manual respectively. Title pages will be prepared in manuscript.

Place	Date	Hour	Summary of Events and Information	Remarks and references to Appendices
Oudezeele (Gunner Map W.10 & 3.b.)	1-10-17 2/10/17 & 3/10/17		Issue of first blankets for men to all units.	F.J.
	7/10/17		Dump stores moved to W. 5. c. 9. 5. Corps stores at Old Dump handed over to 41st Division	F.J.
Coxyde Bains	16/10/17		Office and stores established at Coxyde Bains (M.6 Central) + billets arranged at "Hotel Beausejour". All rearrangements of 66th Divn F.J. + 1st Divn — with exception of 6th Welsh Regt — transferred to 41st Division for administration.	F.J.
do	17/10/17 11am		A.D.O.S. XV Corps inspected stores & working.	F.J.
	18/10/17		D.A.D.O.S. visited Divisional Battalion at Corps Training Camp & Divisional Rest School & made purchases of stores — watching 1 Singer Sewing Machine for 1/8th Lanc. Fusiliers — at Dunkirk	F.J.
	19/10/17		Second Blankets per man issued to Divisions & Leahs Jerkins to Infantry F.J. T.

Sheet 2.

WAR DIARY
or
INTELLIGENCE SUMMARY.
(Erase heading not required.)

Army Form C. 2118.

Instructions regarding War Diaries and Intelligence Summaries are contained in F. S. Regs., Part II. and the Staff Manual respectively. Title pages will be prepared in manuscript.

Place	Date	Hour	Summary of Events and Information	Remarks and references to Appendices
Aryshe Ponins	23/10/17		6 Sighting telescopes No 4 Special received for Artillery Observation Posts. Armourer Staff Sergeant to Gallery injured it Armourer Shop by defective blow lamp & admitted to Hospital	F.9.
	27/10/17		1 Private, A.O.Corps joined from Paris to instruct men from Infantry Battalions in repairing gum boots.	F.9.
	28/10/17.		7 men from Infantry & R.A. joined for instruction in gum boot repairing	F.9.
	29/10/17.		8 Category "B" Infantrymen joined from base to relieve A.O.C. men of Category "A"	F.9.
	31/10/17		A.D.O.S. visited A.D.O.S. XV Corps with reference to Anti-aircraft Sights on Machine Guns, & return of gum boots to Base.	F.9.

SECRET

War Diary

of

D.A.D.O.S. 42nd Division

November 1917

Army Form C. 2118.

WAR DIARY
or
~~INTELLIGENCE SUMMARY.~~
(Erase heading not required.)

D.A.D.O.S.
42ND
(E.L.) DIVISION.
No ....
Date 3/12/17

November 1917

Instructions regarding War Diaries and Intelligence Summaries are contained in F. S. Regs., Part II. and the Staff Manual respectively. Title pages will be prepared in manuscript.

Place	Date	Hour	Summary of Events and Information	Remarks and references to Appendices
Craywel Bruno	1-11-17		DADOS visited Base Depot 135 Bde re clothing and equipment, also the 2nd and 45 OMW(L) with reference to repair of firing mechanism of Heavy Mortar (Stokes).	F.9.
	2-11-17		Visited ADMS 15th Corps, and I/5 F.A. with regard to return of unserviceable clothing.	F.9.
	3-11-17		Had trouble brought for treatment of French Heat.	F.9.
	4-11-17		Arrangements made with IV Army Heavy Mobile Workshop for the manufacturing of 100 brass studs for regulation of depression and elevation on dials of Vickers Guns.	F.9.
	5-11-17		Visited Divisional Wing, inspected QMs dump.	F.9.
	6-11-17		Conference with A.DOS with reference to the reduction of establishment in vehicles and harness. Proposal arranged. The question of replacement of category A men was also discussed.	F.9.
	7-11-17		Stops collected from MMGC and Vickers Guns of 124 Mn Gun Coy. completed with studs and chains. Ascertained from Light Mobile Shop reason as to removal of 1 Blanquer and bomication from Walter Cart Mark II.	F.9.
	8-11-17.		Attended conference at 9th Divisional Headquarters to arrange for the clearance of Ordnance Stores on vacation of area by British troops.	F.9.
	9-11-17.		Site selected on Light Railway for Dump of Trench and Area Stores being returned.	F.9.

Army Form C. 2118.

Sheet 2 — WAR DIARY
or
INTELLIGENCE SUMMARY.
(Erase heading not required.)

Instructions regarding War Diaries and Intelligence Summaries are contained in F.S. Regs., Part II. and the Staff Manual respectively. Title pages will be prepared in manuscript.

Place	Date	Hour	Summary of Events and Information	Remarks and references to Appendices
Coxyde Bains	10-11-17		13 G.S. wagons, 1 mess-cart, surplus harness & saddlery of D.A.C sent to railhead adjustments for transmission to Base	F.1.9.
	11-11-17		Arrangements made with Officer i/c light Railway for supply of trucks for clearing french stores to railhead.	F.1.9.
	12-11-17		Visited D.A.D.O.S. with reference to the return of 9.45 french mortars to Base, and also cancellation of outstanding indents for spare parts etc	F.1.9.
	14-11-17		New area visited with D.A.Q.G.	F.1.9.
	16-11-17		Clearing of Area & Corps Stores proceeding satisfactorily, already several trucks consigned to Base.	F.1.9.
	17-11-17		Lewis Guns issued to Brigades for Instructional Purposes returned to O.O. Corps troops. Arm.S/Sgt Moore returned from duty at XV Corps Lewis Gun School.	F.1.9.
	18-11-17		Two Machine Gun Detection issued by IV Corps Troops.	F.1.9.
Aire-sur-la-Lys	19-11-17		Offices and Stores moved to Aire-sur-la-Lys, under XI Corps.	F.1.9.
	20-11-17		Position of Workshops, Army M.T.s, Gun Park ascertained from O.O. 15th Corps troops	F.1.9.
	21-11-17		Brigade Dumps, inspected at Barracks with D.A.D.M.G	F.1.9.

Army Form C. 2118.

Sheet 2

WAR DIARY
INTELLIGENCE SUMMARY.
(Erase heading not required.)

November 1917

Place	Date	Hour	Summary of Events and Information	Remarks and references to Appendices
Aux-sur-Cys	22-11-17		G.O.C. 1st Infantry Bde and OC 1/4 Manchester Regt interviewed reference the painting of Steel Helmets.	Ft.9
	23-11-17		Visited Corps with DAQMG and saw DA, DST and DAQMG 25th Division and discussed "taking over". Inspected Advance refilling points, and made arrangements for the handing over of Corps and area stores.	Ft.9
	25-11-17		Alterations to Beds of Vickers tripods carried out in Armourers shop. AOO visited at Fismes, re procedure of obtaining stores from 1st Army Gun Park.	Ft.9
	28-11-17		Armourers and Shoemakers shops moved to Fism.	Ft.9
Fism.	29-11-17		Offices and stores opened at Fism.	Ft.9
	30-11-17		La Gorgue Railhead moved and system arranged of transferring Ordnance stores to Steenwerck Trucks. Route into Salvage Dump and huts at refilling points inspected in conjunction with RE and necessary repairs arranged.	Ft.9

Vol 11

War Diary

D.A.D.O.S. 42nd Division

December 1914.

D.A.D.O.S.
42ND
(E.L.) DIVISION.
No
Date 2-1-17

Army Form C. 2118.

Sheet 1

WAR DIARY
INTELLIGENCE SUMMARY.
(Erase heading not required.)

Instructions regarding War Diaries and Intelligence Summaries are contained in F. S. Regs., Part II. and the Staff Manual respectively. Title pages will be prepared in manuscript.

Place	Date	Hour	Summary of Events and Information	Remarks and references to Appendices
Loos	1-12-19	—	A DOS 15th Corps called. Visited 1st Army Gun Park with DADMG to ascertain method of obtaining stores. Interviewed lytn 1st Army Heavy Mobile workshop, and also visited 42nd Divisional Wing with reference to stores required.	A/9
	2-12-19	—	All AA lights and mountings for Lewis and Vickers Guns overhauled in Armourers Shop prior to issuing to units. Clothing and Salvage Dumps inspected.	A/9
	5-12-19	—	Attended conference of Staff Captains of Brigades with AA & QMG and DADMG. with reference to supply of Ordnance Stores generally, the working of Divisional Baths, Ammunition Dump and Canteen. 4000 leather jerkins issued.	A/9
	6-12-19	—	Woollen gloves and sheepskin lined coats issued.	A/9
	7-12-19	—	Clean clothing store at Loos inspected, also lock and shirt repairing depôts.	A/9
	8-12-19	—	Forward Salvage Dump, and Gum Boot drying store inspected. Visited 06 1/9 Manchester Regt. re outstanding stores	A/9
	10-12-19	—	Piping for Lewis Gun mountings collected from R.E. dump at Loos, and also sticks for the manufacture of tripods for musketry instruction at Divisional Wing. Visited Staff Captain 124 Bde., with reference to outstanding stores.	A/9 A/9

Army Form C. 2118.

WAR DIARY Sheet 2

INTELLIGENCE SUMMARY.

(Erase heading not required.)

Place	Date	Hour	Summary of Events and Information	Remarks and references to Appendices
Locon	11-12-19		Sheepskin - lined coats issued to M.J. Driver.	JFS
	16-12-19		Visited 125 Bde HQrts, and interviewed Brigadier General and Staff Captain, who stated that the only complaint was lack of pants.	JFS
	19-12-19		Visited OC 1/4 Lanic Fusrs, referred him to JOM 1st Army (U.), as to repairs to travelling kitchen. Two OML 9.45" Mortars issued to D/142 Trench Mortar Battery vide 1st Army OS 9264 df. 11/12. Two 4.5" Howitzers and carriages issued to D/210 Field Arty Bde. and one 4.5" How and carriage to D/211 Field Arty Bde. to replace three handed over to 21st Division on joining First Army. One 4.5" Howitzer of D/210 RFA and two 4.5" Howitzers of D/211 RFA provisionally condemned under QMG 208 (Q.B.3) df. 10/12 but to remain in action.	JFS
	24-12-19		Visited Corps with DAQG, also 1st Army Gun Park. One 4.5" How of D/210 RFA provisionally condemned under QMG. 208 (Q.B.3). df. 10-12-19.	JFS
	26-12-19		Two 18 pdr. guns of D/210. RFA provisionally condemned under QMG. 208 (Q.B.3) df. 16/12/19 but to remain in action until finally condemned.	JFS
	28-12-19		Dial sights and Lewis Gun Parts collected from Gun Park.	JFS
	29-12-19		Adjutant and Quartermaster of 1/4 Manchester Regt interviewed reference outstanding stores. No complaints.	JFS
	30-12-19		In. Gloves & Shields hand for motor cyclists issued to supply Column.	JFS
	31-12-19		Visited ADOS 1st Corps reference report of Chaffcutters, and also transfer of units administered by me, although not 1st Corps units	JFS

War Diary

January 1918.

D.A.D.O.S. 42nd Division.

Army Form C. 2118.

WAR DIARY
or
INTELLIGENCE SUMMARY.
(Erase heading not required.)

Sheet 1

D.A.D.O.S.
42ND
(E.L.) DIVISION

Instructions regarding War Diaries and Intelligence Summaries are contained in F. S. Regs., Part II. and the Staff Manual respectively. Title pages will be prepared in manuscript.

Place	Date	Hour	Summary of Events and Information	Remarks and references to Appendices
Locon	2-1-18		Issued Sacks for Bayonet Fighting to 2nd Div Wing	App.1
	4-1-18		Visited No 1 Gun Park to settle question of Carriage W/S' Iron. Stated to be outstanding for D/210 R.F.A. 14th, 68th and 69th (Chinese) Labour Companies transferred to OC. 15th Corps Troops D/Special Coy RE transferred to OO 4th Army Troops Fo 3. Stock and Dies handed from 186 Heavy Mobile Shops, for alteration to screws of Pet Food Containers. Alterations to rifles with cut-offs being carried out in Divisional Armourer's Shop under G.R.O. 2964.	App.1
	5-1-18		Visited I Corps Salvage Dump with Divisional Salvage Officer. Serviceable Web Equipment, bicycle parts and wirecutters taken over for issue. HQ 33 Labour Group and 436 Employment Coy transferred to OO 15 Corps Troops. Repayment Stores not required handed over to No.1 Army Clothing Depot Bethune	App.1
	6-1-18		18 pair No 2630 Boots finally condemned by Lieut. Col OMW(L)	App.1
	7-1-18		40 Steel Helmets with Visors (Improved Pattern) issued on trial to Division — 10 to each Infantry Bde, 5 to QA, 5 to RE — Carriage 18 Pdr A/No 24316 with Sight Rocking Bar condemned by Lt Col. OMW(Arty).	App.1
	8-1-18		Two 18 pdr tires 667 and 2697 collected from Gun Park and delivered to Lieut Col OMW(L) for 13/210 Bde RFA. Divisional RE complete with 18 pairs. Visited 42nd Divl Salvage Dump, & took over serviceable stores, including Steel Helmets (badly not serviceable)	App.1

Army Form C. 2118.

D.A.D.O.S.
4280

Instructions regarding War Diaries and Intelligence Summaries are contained in F. S. Regs., Part II. and the Staff Manual respectively. Title pages will be prepared in manuscript.

WAR DIARY
or
INTELLIGENCE SUMMARY.
(Erase heading not required.)

Sheet 2

Place	Date	Hour	Summary of Events and Information	Remarks and references to Appendices
Rouen	8-1-18		Interviewed Staff Capt. R.A. reference outstanding guns and gun stores.	Fr. 9
	9-1-18		84 Army Field Artillery Bde formed from OO 4th Army Troops No 2. A, B & C - 18pdr Batteries, D How Battery got in touch with adjutant of Bde, & with Staff Capt R.A. made note of principal outstanding gun stores. D Bty deficient one 4.5" How. Reviewed outstanding indents of A/84 a Fr Bde with Quartermaster and OC Battery.	Fr. 9
	10-1-18		Interviewed all QM's of 84 & A/Bde, and reviewed outstanding indents, principal stores required hastened from Base, and indents for gun parts to complete submitted to No 1 Ord Gun Park. Collected wire cutters for ORe from 1st Corps Salvage Re-issuing Store Berry. Tables and forms collected from D.A.D.O.S 46th Division.	Fr. 9
	11-1-18		Three tons stores for 84 A Fr Bde collected by lorry from OO 4th Army Troops at Amiens.	Fr. 9
	12-1-18		4.5" Howitzer No 430 and 1857 of 9/84 A Fr Bde provisionally condemned under QMG 208 (QB3) of 10-12-17, but to remain in action till finally condemned.	Fr. 9
	13-1-18		Visited ROD railhead, serviceable web Equipment collected for re-issue.	Fr. 9

WAR DIARY
or
INTELLIGENCE SUMMARY.

(Erase heading not required.)

Army Form C. 2118.

Sheet 3.

Place	Date	Hour	Summary of Events and Information	Remarks and references to Appendices
Rouen	14-1-18		Alteration of butt catches for Lewis Guns, commencing in Divisional Armourers Shop vide G.R.O. 3047. 1st Army wired reference two 4·5" Howitzers of 84 A.F.A. Bde provisionally condemned on 12th inst. None at present available for replacement. Gun parts for 84 A.F.A. Bde collected from Gun Park.	J.1.9.
	16-1-18		Visited 1st Heavy Mobile Workshop reference repair of Stombos items and sharpening of Blades of Power Horse clipping machines.	J.1.9.
	17-1-18		251 Tunnelling Coy R.E. transferred to 42nd Division for Ordnance Services by OO 15th Corps Troops. Entrained D/B D/84 A.F.A. Bde. reference outstanding indents. Lt Col. W. Chester-Bram. ADOS 1st Corps paid a visit, and arranged disposal of surplus G.S. wagons sent in error.	J.1.9.
	19-1-18		Visited Artillery Dump with DA.Q.M.G. and inspected 4·5" How and 18 pdr ammunition. No 266 In.C. Coy joined Division, making 4th Company – strength 10 officers 197 O.Rs and 66 horses. Repair of Hot Food Containers being carried out in Armourers Shop.	J.1.9.

Army Form C. 2118.

WAR DIARY
INTELLIGENCE SUMMARY
(Erase heading not required.)

Sheet 4

Place	Date	Hour	Summary of Events and Information	Remarks and references to Appendices
Lozon	20-1-18		Attended conference of D.A.D.s.O at 1st Corps Headquarters. The question of the disbandment of 3 Battalions was discussed, and it was agreed that a clearance depôt should be established at Bergvette under an Ordnance Officer for the return of all Equipment held on G1098 and other special surplus stores, and other special surplus stores, will be returned to 9.00 of the formation concerned. The 51st Division will detail one O.R an A/S man for duty at the clearance depôt. Air cylinders, stores, tools and Stewart machine stopping heads collected from 1st A.m Workshop.	F.S.
	21-1-18		Two armourers detailed to inspect all rifles of 125 Infantry Bde commencing on those of 1/6 Lanc. Fus. Arrangements made for repairing of Gum Boots in Bootmaker's shop. Inspected Divisional Salvage Dump.	F.S.
	22-1-18		Visited H.Qrs 84 Army Field Artillery Bde, and interviewed adjutant regarding completion of batteries with 9 in Sights, telescopes, and chaffcutters. Two chaffcutters required to complete issued from stock. Visited D/311 RFA and No 1 Coy 43nd Divisional Train with J.Om No 1 Order (Inspector) for the purpose of valuing privately owned chaffcutters, to be taken over by the Government. Inspected Gun Salvage Dump at Bethune. Arrived from RTO Bethune that nine surplus G.S.wagons had been cleared. 5 issued and 4 returned to Base.	F.S.

Army Form C. 2118.

WAR DIARY
INTELLIGENCE SUMMARY.
(Erase heading not required.)

Sheet 5

Place	Date	Hour	Summary of Events and Information	Remarks and references to Appendices
Béthune	22-1-18		6 turn Boot repairs commenced work under supervision of the Bergt Shoemaker	F3
	23-1-18		Visited A Sgt 1st Corps regarding the transfer of five units, not in area, but ordnanced by me. Matter to be taken up with 15th Corps Five Lump Lines issued to Divisional wing for Instructional purposes. Interviewed Staff Captain 195 Infantry Bde reference position as regards main outstanding items. Visited 1st Light Mobile Workshop. 432 Field Coy RE transferred to 55th Division for Ordnance Services	F3
	24-1-18		Discussed disbandment of Infantry Battalions with AA & QMG. Visited Bomy and inspected Offices and Stores of DADOS 55th Division in view of pending move, also called on Divl Supply Column on return journey	F3
	25-1-18		Interviewed 268th M.G. Coy, and ascertained they were well equipped and had no complaints. Also visited No.1 Sect. D.A.C. and inspected QM's stores; no complaints. Arranged with Staff Capt 125Bde to overhaul Lewis Guns of 1/5 and 1/6 Lancs Fusrs in Armourers Shop. Armourers Staff Sergt Storey & Berry reported that all rifles of 125 Bde had been inspected and reports rendered to Staff Captain.	F3
	26-1-18		Visited 6th Lancs Fusrs at Terre du Roi and visited QM's store with Adjutant and QM, discussed the importance of the return of all unserviceable clothing. Visited 7th Lancs Fusrs at Beuvry, and also inspected QM's stores.	F3

Army Form C. 2118.

WAR DIARY
or
INTELLIGENCE SUMMARY.
(Erase heading not required.)

Sheet 6

Instructions regarding War Diaries and Intelligence Summaries are contained in F. S. Regs., Part II. and the Staff Manual respectively. Title pages will be prepared in manuscript.

Place	Date	Hour	Summary of Events and Information	Remarks and references to Appendices
Rouen	26-1-18.		Inspected QM's store of 1/5th Lancs Fus. at Wingette. Arrangements made to take a man as learner in the Armourer Shop for minor repairs of bicycles and rifles. Eight Lewis Guns of 5th Lancs Fus. overhauled in Armourer Shop & remaining rifles called in.	
	27-1-18.		DADOS 55th Division visited for the purpose of inspecting stores and offices with a view to taking over in the near future. Inspected clean stocking at Berne with DAQ, and watched Jocks shot at work, and the sacking of dirty clothing for return to Abbeville Laundry. Inspected QM Stores of 1/9 Manchester Regt, and noticed that unit was holding to large a stock of clothing etc, and reported this fact to AA & QMG.	
	28-1-18.		Two Machine Gun Detectors returned to Base. Stores delivered to OC 15th Corps Troops for units recently transferred. All machine guns of 1/5 and 1/6 Lancs Fus. overhauled and returned to units. Armourer reports forwarded to HQrs 125 Bde.	
	29-1-18.		Capt Potter RE left for Ammunition Course at the 14 Ordnance Depot	
	30-1-18.		Lieut W.J. Kinnage. AOD arrived for temporary duty as acting DADOS	

WA/3

War Diary

D.A.D.O.S. 42nd Div:

February. 1918.

1. D.A.D.O.S.
42nd
(T.L.) DIVISION.

Army Form C. 2118.

WAR DIARY
or
INTELLIGENCE SUMMARY.

(Erase heading not required.)

Instructions regarding War Diaries and Intelligence Summaries are contained in F. S. Regs., Part II. and the Staff Manual respectively. Title pages will be prepared in manuscript.

Place	Date	Hour	Summary of Events and Information	Remarks and references to Appendices
Rouen	1-2-18	—	Arrangements made with Divl Artillery to make jackets from baling for the use of personnel engaged in handling shell, and so protect S.D. clothing	AF9.
	6-2-18	—	Lt. W.J. Turnage AOD left for duty with 4th Division.	AF9
	9-2-18	—	Lewis Guns of 1/6 Manchester Regt overhauled in Divisional Armourers Shop	AF9
	10-2-18	—	Visited Busnes to see DADOS 33rd Div: reference taking over of Offices and stores	AF9
Busnes	13-2-18	—	Went to Busnes, and established D.A.D. offices and dump; also Armourers Shop, Shoemakers shop, and unserviceable returns store	AF9
	14-2-18	—	Capt L.J. Potter Inf. AOD returned off Ammunition Course on to 4th Ordnance Depot.	AF9
	15-2-18	—	Arrangements made to receive all stores from Disbanded Units, as follows 1/6 Lancs Fus, 1/4 East Lancs, 1/9 Manchester Regt.	AF9
	11-2-18	—	All stores and equipment received from three disbanded units. Dumps and stores inspected by DA & QMG 42 Div. AA & QMG 42 Div paid a visit, also ADOS 1st Corps with reference to returned stores	AF9
	17-2-18	—	Visited RE & filler and arranged for him to despatch stores and equipment to Base Gun Parts collected from No 1 Gun Park	AF9 AF9

D.A.D.O.S.
42nd
(E.L.) DIVISION

Army Form C. 2118.

WAR DIARY
INTELLIGENCE SUMMARY
(Erase heading not required.)

2nd Sheet

Place	Date	Hour	Summary of Events and Information	Remarks and references to Appendices
Busnes.	18.2.18		Visited dumps of 1/5th, 1/4th, 1/8th Lancs Fusiliers, 1/5th, 1/6th, 1/7th, 1/8th, 19th Manchester Regts. 1/5 East Lancs Regiments, and made inspection of same accompanied with A.D.O.S. 1st Corps	F.9
	19.2.18		Visited 42nd Div. Supply Column, also refilling point of 125 Infantry Bde with his Lordns Chetwood, to select site for Ordnance Dump. 125 Bde M.G.s instructed to return all Signalling Equipment of disbanded units. Interviewed O.C. of 1/1 E.L. Field Ambulance, 1/3rd Field Ambulance, also O.C. of Machine Gun Companies. Ascertained from BC & QM of 1/4 Northumberland Fus (Pioneers) what stores were required to complete, informed that they were being reduced to three Companies.	F.9 F.9 F.9
	20.2.18		Stores inspected by D.D.O.S. 1st Army. Items issued for A.A. work used as follows:— Infantry Battalions — 2 each. Field Companies — 1 each Batteries R.F.A. — 1 each.	F.9
	21.2.18		Visited all three refilling points, and made arrangements with the train companies able to erect portable huts at the adjoining dumps, for the protection of stores in wet weather issued D.R.O.	F.9

Army Form C. 2118.

D.A.D.O.S.
42nd

Instructions regarding War Diaries and Intelligence Summaries are contained in F.S. Regs., Part II. and the Staff Manual respectively. Title pages will be prepared in manuscript.

WAR DIARY
~~INTELLIGENCE SUMMARY~~
(Erase heading not required.)

3rd Sheet

Place	Date	Hour	Summary of Events and Information	Remarks and references to Appendices
Busnes	22-2-18		Interviewed C.O. 1/2nd Field Ambulance. 80 Rifles for issue to Machine Gun Corps, on withdrawal of Pistols, obtained from Railhead. Visited DHQ and discussed with C.R.E. the question of Cooks Carts to be issued to Field Companies in lieu of Limber Gd. Instruction given as to indenting and withdrawal of surplus vehicles. Also called on 60 of Divisional Wing. The question of repairs to Guns & vehicles arranged with 10th Ho1 Mobile Workshop (light).	F.9.
	23-2-18		Visited refilling points during issues of stores. Attended lecture on Economy of Government Stores. — Lecturer Col Sypriess A.O.D.	F.9. F.9.
	24-2-18		Statements of deficiencies of stores handed in by three battalions forwarded to A.D.O.S. 1st Corps.	F.9.
	25-2-18		Visited Bouques with object of finding suitable dump, pending a move to more central position truly place required by 1st Army Bus Company.	F.9.

Army Form C. 2118.

WAR DIARY
or
INTELLIGENCE SUMMARY.   4th Sheet
(Erase heading not required.)

Instructions regarding War Diaries and Intelligence Summaries are contained in F. S. Regs., Part II. and the Staff Manual respectively. Title pages will be prepared in manuscript.

Place	Date	Hour	Summary of Events and Information	Remarks and references to Appendices
Busnes	26/2/18		Visited Refilling points and saw QMs of Battalions. Arranged with Staff Capt. 155 Bde. to overhaul all Lewis Guns in Brigade commencing with 1/8 Lancs Fus[iliers] — 8 guns to be sent in at a time. Interviewed Pioneer Battalion with reference to return of surplus stores owing to reduction in establishment. A sight and mounting for Lewis Gun issued to OC Ord. Wing for instructional purposes. Two Stadia Range Indicators issued to D.A.G.O. for trial.	F.J.
	27/2/18		Armourer's report received on inspection of Rifles of 1/4th Manchester Regt. Serviceable 1. Pistols 32 inspected 1 defective. Rifles inspected 137. Defective 58.	F.J.
	28/2/18		Armourer Sergt Major sent to inspect Machine Guns of 4 M.G. Companies. Visited D.A.D.M. and arranged the transfer of vehicles from the surplus transport of 3 Disbanded Battalions, to complete Machine Gun Battalion. Three lorries but surplus to requirements of M.G. B'tn to be transferred to Field Companies. Called on D.D.M.O. with reference to his new establishment, and indents to complete to two 6 gun Batteries. Inspected proposed site for dump at Labourière. Saw OC D/311. Bde R.F.A. re purchase of forage and chaffcutter.	F.J.

SECRET.

Vol 14

War Diary

March 1918

D.A.D.O.S. 42nd Division

1st Sheet

Army Form C. 2118.

WAR DIARY
or
INTELLIGENCE SUMMARY.

Ordnance 42nd Division

Place	Date	Hour	Summary of Events and Information	Remarks and references to Appendices
Busnes	1-3-18	—	100 Rifles & bayonets collected from Railhead for reserve. 50 flat irons for Divisional Baths collected from 1st Heavy Mobile Workshop. Visited D.Y. Inf. re organization of Trench Mortar Batteries, also discussed the question of re-organization of Signal Coy. with DADMS. Eight Lewis Guns of 1/6 Lancs Fus: overhauled.	F.3 F.3 F.3
—	2-3-18		Stores and new billets inspected at Labeuvrere.	F.3
—	3-3-18			
Labeuvrere	4-3-18		Moved offices, stores and shops to Labeuvrere. Rifles of 1/6 Manchester Regt inspected. 481 overhauled, 83 defective, 8 of which were returned to Divil Armourer's Shop for exchange. 14 with dirty barrels, due to neglecting to use gauge after firing.	F.3
—	5-3-18		A.D.O.S. 1st Corps inspected dump. 21 Lewis Guns complete, collected from Gun Park to complete to Scale B of issues from A.A. WDR. Arranged for despatch to Base of surplus boots bars of Tr.C. Companies and Limber R.E. wagons of 3 Field Companies.	F.3 F.3
—	6-3-18		Visited Bng'ade Ordnance refilling points at Annesin, Busnes and Bas Reevre. The complaints from Units.	F.3
—	7-3-18		Issued Discharger Cups for Fus 36 Grenade - initial supply 8 per Infantry and Pioneer Battalion. Interviewed O.C. Bombing School also Adjutants of 210 & 211 Field Arty Bdes, re drawing of Stores from refilling points.	F.3

Army Form C. 2118.

2nd Sheet

WAR DIARY
~~INTELLIGENCE SUMMARY~~

(Erase heading not required.)

Instructions regarding War Diaries and Intelligence Summaries are contained in F. S. Regs., Part II. and the Staff Manual respectively. Title pages will be prepared in manuscript.

Place	Date	Hour	Summary of Events and Information	Remarks and references to Appendices
Lakonnere	9-3-16		Visited refilling points with Officer on probation in Q office. Interviewed Staff Capt. 126 Bde.	A&Q
—"—	10-3-16		400 Trump tunics received from Base, distributed to Division.	A&Q
—"—	11-3-16		All arms of 1/5 Manchester Regt. inspected. General condition fairly good. Rifles 735. Defective 46. Unserviceable 1. Pistols 31. —"— 1. —"— nil. Gun bns 119. —"— 1. —"— nil. Defective repaired in Armourers Shop.	A&Q
—"—	13-3-16		Visited No.1 Heavy Mobile Workshop, and refilling points	A&Q
—"—	14-3-16		Arranged collection of Tents, Tables and Forms from No.1 Gun Park. Visited DADOS 11th Division at La Bourse. 56 Binoculars for 1st & 2nd Lights handed over to DADM No.1 Order Mobile Workshop(?) and arranged to send in 6 sights at a time from Batteries	A&Q
—"—	17-3-16		Inspected Bombing School and was instructed in handling of new discharger cup for the 31 Grenade	A&Q
—"—	18-3-16		Visited refilling points, issues proceeding smoothly.	A&Q

3rd Sheet

Army Form C. 2118.

WAR DIARY
INTELLIGENCE SUMMARY.

(Erase heading not required.)

Instructions regarding War Diaries and Intelligence Summaries are contained in F.S. Regs., Part II. and the Staff Manual respectively. Title pages will be prepared in manuscript.

Place	Date	Hour	Summary of Events and Information	Remarks and references to Appendices
Lauvriero	20-3-18		Received six Hotchkiss guns for issue to Train Companies, to Y Coy and Employment Coy.	F.9
—	21-3-18		Called on 428 Field Coy RE. at Le Quesnoy & inspected R.E. limber. Interviewed 16 SAA Section RAB and 3rd Train Headquarters. Twenty pairs binoculars, rendered surplus by formation of Machine Gun Bn., returned to Base through R.O.O Lillers. Light trench mortar taken to 1st 9.S.M.W. for repair.	F.9
—	22-3-18		Selected new refilling point for 124 Brigade. Snap reference (continued sheet) V.28. a.9.2. Twelve hours notice to move, orders received at 8 pm.	F.9
Basseux	23-3-18		Moved with four lorries to Basseux. Joined Divl. Corps. Surplus stores, shoemakers tools, etc left in charge of two men at Lauvrieres.	F.9
—	24-3-18		Divl. Headquarters to Adinfer. Transferred outstanding indents to Southern Base.	F.9
—	25-3-18		Divl. Headquarters to Monchy-au-Bois	F.9
St. Amand	26-3-18		Moved to St. Amand. Joined IV Corps. Disbanded Armourers & Shoemakers shops owing to new phase in operations. One armourer only retained.	F.9
	27-3-18		Visited AAS IV Corps. Received 10 Vickers Guns complete, also 44 Lewis Guns complete from OO IV Corps troops. Issued in replacement of casualties.	F.9

Army Form C. 2118.

A.H. Sheet

Instructions regarding War Diaries and Intelligence Summaries are contained in F. S. Regs., Part II. and the Staff Manual respectively. Title pages will be prepared in manuscript.

WAR DIARY
or
INTELLIGENCE SUMMARY.
(Erase heading not required.)

Place	Date	Hour	Summary of Events and Information	Remarks and references to Appendices
St Amand	28-3-18		12 Vickers Guns received from O.O. IV Corps troops, and issued to replace casualties	FS9
—	29-3-18		DHQ to St Amand. Collected 100 B.L. Tents and 150 French Shelters for Artillery and Transport lines	FS9
Beaurepaire	30-3-18		Moved to Beaurepaire to prepare dump for refitting. Forward issuing dump established at St Amand	FS9
—	31-3-18		Six Trucks of Divisional Bath and Brigade Dump Stores received at Doullens from Bethune. All cleared and stored by 5 p.m.	FS9

Secret
YA/15

War Diary

D.A.D.O.S. 42nd Division

April 1918

Army Form C. 2118.

Sheet 1.

WAR DIARY
~~INTELLIGENCE SUMMARY.~~

(Erase heading not required.)

Instructions regarding War Diaries and Intelligence Summaries are contained in F. S. Regs., Part II. and the Staff Manual respectively. Title pages will be prepared in manuscript.

D.A.D.O.S.
42ND
F.L.D DIVISION.
No April 1918.
Date

Place	Date	Hour	Summary of Events and Information	Remarks and references to Appendices
Beaurepaire	3-4-18		Forward dump established at Henu, one W/O with two storemen to same. Visited A.D.of IV Corps and OO IV Corps troops.	FFS
	4-4-18		Called at Gun Park, Bruay - le Chateau to ascertain if a stock of Sno 36 Rifle Grenade Discharger was held. Demanded same on Base, as no stock was held. Inquiries made regarding position as to supply of Elephants AA sights for Kevos and Norclum Guns.	FFS
	6-4-18		30 sets of packsaddlery with 60 water carriers received from IV Corps troops. Issued 10 sets to each infantry Bde.	FFS
Pas	4-4-18		Offices and dump to Pas, for reopening of Division. Issued 16 Lewis Guns to 118 Lewis Gunners to replace lost in action	FFS FFS
	14-4-18		Instructions received to vacate Sercus Le ville Pas, as it is required to accommodate IV Corps troops	FFS
	15-4-18			FFS
Bours	16-4-18		Dump and offices moved to Bours on relief of 34th Division	FFS
	17-4-18		Called on A.D.of IV Corps regarding lights & Warnings for Lewis Guns employed on A.A. duties, also reserve of 400 units to be held for Mustard Gas Casualties	FFS
	18-4-18		Six Lewis Guns received from Gun Park for issue in case of emergency. 400 suits demanded ft gas cases, to be handed over to incoming Division on relief.	FFS
	19-4-18		Thirty Lewis Guns received from Gun Park as further reserve to meet immediate requirements. Visited railhead Walincourt with D.A.Q.G., and arranged with RTO for allotment of trucks daily for salvage.	FFS

F.H. Finch, O/C 42 M.T. Coy. Reference Lorries.

Army Form C. 2118.

WAR DIARY
or
INTELLIGENCE SUMMARY.
(Erase heading not required.)

Instructions regarding War Diaries and Intelligence Summaries are contained in F. S. Regs., Part II. and the Staff Manual respectively. Title pages will be prepared in manuscript.

Sheet 2

D.A.D.O.S.
42ND
(E.L.) DIVISION

Place	Date	Hour	Summary of Events and Information	Remarks and references to Appendices
Couin	19-4-18		Rear dump at Beauquesne inspected. Visited 42 Divisional Rest Camp at Marieux, reserve equipment of Reinforcements	
	20-4-18		All Battalion Dumps inspected, and arranged that all Ordnance Stores to be taken over condemned, serviceable to be re-issued, and unserviceable to be returned to Base. Visited Railhead, everything satisfactory.	
	21-4-18		Report on Battalion dumps submitted to AA & QMG. Six Lewis Guns issued to Camp Commdts BHQ for protection of Chateau against hostile aircraft.	
	25-4-18		Barrage No 198 & 40 of 2/210 condemned for wear and shell fire.	
	28-4-18		Barrage No 1306 of 2/29b condemned shell fire. Six stocks of Blankets to Base. Parallescope received from Corps Troops for trial. Issued to A/210 Bde R.F.A.	
	29-4-18		Visited Railhead with reference to getting further trucks for despatch of Winter Clothing.	
	30-4-18		Special Anti-Rust mounting received from OC IV Corps Troops for distribution in the line. 150 Gas Rattles for distribution in the line.	

Secret

Vol. 6.

War Diary

of

D.A.D.O.S. 42nd Division

May 1918.

D.A.D.O.S.
31 MAY 1918
42ND (E. LANCS.) DIV.

Army Form C. 2118.

WAR DIARY
INTELLIGENCE SUMMARY.
(Erase heading not required.)

Sheet 1

42ND
(E.L.) DIVISION

Instructions regarding War Diaries and Intelligence Summaries are contained in F. S. Regs., Part II. and the Staff Manual respectively. Title pages will be prepared in manuscript.

Place	Date	Hour	Summary of Events and Information	Remarks and references to Appendices
Couin	3-5-18	—	Visited D.A.D.O.S. 54th Division, reference taking over from him. Arrangements made with R.O.O. Warlincourt for despatch of Winter Clothing to Base.	279
	4-5-18	—	Advanced party to Pas to pitch store tents.	279
Pas.	5-5-18	—	Offices and dump moved to Pas. 4.5" Howitzer and barrage Nos. 3526 and 13061, also 4.5" Nos. No 2493 condemned, chest fire.	279
	6-5-18	—	Capt. J.J. Potter. 2nd. A.O.D. terrecied on seven days special leave to U.K. Ord. Q.F. 18 pdr. of C/210 Bde R.F.A condemned for wear, handed to 5th 109th W.	279
	7-5-18	—	Five Americans withdrawn from Battalions, and Divisional Armourer Shop reformed. Shoemaker's Shop also re-established.	279
	9-5-18	—	6" Newton Mortar No 214 of Y/142 T.M.B. condemned as beyond local repair.	279
	13-5-18	—	Capt. J.J. Potter. M.B.A.O.D. rejoined off leave.	279
	14-5-18	—	304th Infantry Battalion of 77th American Division joined 42nd Division for "training". Arrangements made with Supply Officer, for the attachment of one officer and two other ranks for Ordnance Services. Issue — to "heutons" of 59th French Mortar Batteries returned to Base. Complete with equipment. 5 complete issued to 54th Division. 1 Barrel issued Y/42 T.M.B. 6 complete with other surplus equipment returned to Base.	279

Army Form C. 2118.

WAR DIARY
INTELLIGENCE SUMMARY. Sheet 2
(Erase heading not required.)

Instructions regarding War Diaries and Intelligence Summaries are contained in F. S. Regs., Part II. and the Staff Manual respectively. Title pages will be prepared in manuscript.

D.A.D.O.S. 42ND (E.L.) DIVISION

Place	Date	Hour	Summary of Events and Information	Remarks and references to Appendices
Pas.	15-5-18	–	Interviewed A.D.O.S. IVth Corps, discussed system of administration for prisoners services for American troops. Rear dump at Beaurepaire cleared. 36 Lewis Guns issued under Army Instructions, returned to No. 3. Gun Park. Ord QF 18 pdr. No. 1008.9 of B/295 Bde RFA condemned, sheel fire.	A9
—	16-5-18		Visited A.D.V.S. IVth Corps with D.A.Q.M.G. on matters appertaining to American Regt attached. 3rd Army Inspector of Small Arms, called and arranged to inspect units of Division. Ord QF 18 pdr. Fn. 3346 condemned for scoring (B/295 Bde RFA) Ord QF 18 pdr. No 3410. and Carriage No 6442.3 condemned shell fire (C/210 Bde RFA)	A9
—	18-5-18.		Ord QF 18 pdr. No 6192. condemned, scoring (A/295 Bde R.F.A.)	A9
—	19-5-18		"Monkey Puzzle" AA mountings for Lewis Guns issued to 125 and 126 Bdes for trial.	A9
—	20-5-18		Visited 305th American Field Ambce., with attached American Officer, with reference to issue of stores. Carriage 15 pdr. No 2068 of A/295. condemned, shell fire	A9
—	21-5-18		Rifles of detachments inspected	A9

Army Form C. 2118.

WAR DIARY

~~INTELLIGENCE~~ SUMMARY.

(Erase heading not required.)

3rd Sheet

Instructions regarding War Diaries and Intelligence Summaries are contained in F. S. Regs., Part II. and the Staff Manual respectively. Title pages will be prepared in manuscript.

Place	Date	Hour	Summary of Events and Information	Remarks and references to Appendices
Pas	25-5-18		All personnel including Armourer & MT driver went through Gas Chamber. Ord. QF 18 pdr No 353 of A/296 Bde RFA condemned & boxing.	AF9
-,-	26-5-18		Visited militia with supply officer of 30th Regt, and 2nd Bn 30th Regt at Henu.	AF9
-,-	27-5-18		Barrage 18 pdr. No 96 of A/296 Bde. RFA condemned & sent to 2nd AMW. D.D.O 3rd Army and ADOS 4th Corps inspected Armourers and Shoemakers Shops also Brigade Stores. All Infantry Battalions completed with Lewis Guns to scale 'E'.	AF9
-,-	28-5-18		Ord. QF 18 pdr. No 2451 and Barrage 99348 of B/210 Bde RFA condemned for premature. Barrage 18 pdr. No 26055 of B/210 Bde RFA condemned for repair at 9th W. Inspection of Ammunition from 3rd Army, reported completion of inspection of arms. Inspected rear dump with DAQMG, and arranged to clear unserviceable Field Forge, and other stores to Base.	AF9
-,-	29-5-18		Interviewed Staff Capt. 12th Infantry Bde., discussed question of transport for extra Lewis Guns. Field Kitchens inspected, and one sent in to No 28 OMW(R) for repair. Inspected Armourers, Shoemakers & Tailors Shops of H.Q 7th G.13 Bn., & found everything satisfactory. Interviewed OC 1/6 Manchester Regt.	AF9
-,-	31-5-18		Lethal men by Cpl. Crutter, AOC 4th Corps. to supply and Ordnance Officer at 250 sets of Rochre harness supplied were returned to OC 3rd Army Troops No 4 Ancre le Château.	AF9

SECRET.

Vol 17

D.A.D.O.S.
1 JUL 1918
42ND (E. LANCS.) DIV.

War Diary

of

D.A.D.O.S. 42nd Division

June 1918.

Army Form C. 2118.

WAR DIARY
or
INTELLIGENCE SUMMARY.
(Erase heading not required.)

Instructions regarding War Diaries and Intelligence Summaries are contained in F. S. Regs., Part II. and the Staff Manual respectively. Title pages will be prepared in manuscript.

D.A.D.O.S. 42ND E.A.N DIVISION

Place	Date	Hour	Summary of Events and Information	Remarks and references to Appendices
Pas-en-Artois	2-6-18		Visited Bur-les-Artois to arrange taking over of Dump and Offices of D.A.D.O.S 1/3 Division. Interviewed Brig General 125 Bde. and arranged that W.O. should visit b.0s of Battalions every Wednesday reporting progress, afterwards, to Bde HQ.	F19
	3-6-18		Saw Staff Capt 39th DA with reference to transfer of his units to DA 907 42nd Division for Ordnance Services. Two German Machine Guns returned to No 1 Gun Park	F19
	4-6-18		Interviewed ADOS 11th Corps with reference to the supply of stores to Inf Coy of 39th American Infantry Regt. Visited 304th Inf 4 Coy and D.6 304th Stokes Mortar Platoon, and discussed method of supply of stores and Ammunition. 10t Blanket returned to Base.	F19
	5-6-18.		Gas officer inspected Bde Respirator of detachment. Inspected Rear Dump at Navens with D.A.Q.M.G	F19
	6-6-18.		Transferred American Units to 4th Army. British Rifles, Machine Guns, Vantage handed in before departure.	F19
	7-6-18.		Lewis and Vickers Guns returned to No 3 Gun Park Dump and offices moved to Bus-les-Artois & took over school for alter-	F19 F19
Bus-les-Artois	8-6-18.		Rifles, Bayonets etc collected from American troops, returned to 39th Division by lorries	F19

Army Form C. 2118.

WAR DIARY
INTELLIGENCE SUMMARY.
(Erase heading not required.)

Sheet 2

Instructions regarding War Diaries and Intelligence Summaries are contained in F.S. Regs., Part II. and the Staff Manual respectively. Title pages will be prepared in manuscript.

Place	Date	Hour	Summary of Events and Information	Remarks and references to Appendices
Bus-les-Artois	9-6-18		Visited D.A.D.O.S. H.Q Division at Pas, and also railhead Orville. Met M.F.S Squad. going from Ordnance H.Q Division.	FF8
—	10-6-18		Visited 127 Bde HQ at Souby-au-Bois, with DAQMG — also went to 126 Bde HQ at Gilencourt. Interviewed Staff Captains.	FF8
—	11-6-18		Interviewed O.C. Nº 28 O.M.W. (Light) with reference to the repair of Carts, Water Tank. Also visited 16 MT Coy with reference to supply of stores.	FF8
—	12-6-18		Inspected QMG Stores, Transport lines, Shoemakers' and Tailors' Shops of 126 Brigade. Found everything satisfactory and reported accordingly to AA&QMG.	FF8
—	13-6-18		Similar inspection made of QMG stores, etc, of 1/5, 1/6, 1/7 Manchester Regt, found all in order.	FF8
—			Comparative Statements of Issues of Clothing and boots, also returns of like articles, for 5 months ending 31st May, rendered to all L.O.C.	FF9
—	14-6-18		Inspected with AA&QMG, Transport lines of HQ and 1/29 Field Companies, also 1st & 2nd Field Ambulance	FF9
—	15-6-18		Issued 36 Lewis Guns to Infantry Bns to complete to scale "F", i.e. 28 Guns Exclusive of A.A. Guns.	FF8

Army Form C. 2118.

WAR DIARY
or
INTELLIGENCE SUMMARY.
(Erase heading not required.)

Week 3

Place	Date	Hour	Summary of Events and Information	Remarks and references to Appendices
Bus-les-Artois	16-6-18		Inspected Transport lines of 1/8 Lyres Hsars.	FS
—	17-6-18		With D.A.Q.M.G. visited S.A.A. dumps between Bourcelles and Bailly	FS
—	18-6-18		6" Howitzer of Y/142 T.M.B. (No 22494) condemned B.L.R. and replacement demanded	FS
—	19-6-18		Inspected Clean Clothing Store at Forceville and Baths at Bertrancourt. Visited Salvage Dumps at both places.	FS
—	20-6-18		6" Trench Mortar ZCI (No 2394) issued to Y/142 T.M.B.	FS
—	21-6-18		Visited 11th Machine Gun Squadron. Inspected new Forced Ammunition Dump.	FS
—	23-6-18		Called on D.A.D.O.S. 62nd Division. Seven horse clippers, new pattern, with two guard issued for trial and report.	FS
—	24-6-18		4.5" Howitzer No 2394 and carriage 84998 of B/211 Bde R.F.A. destroyed by hostile shell fire. Replaced by 4.5" How 2863 and carriage no 13155. 1st Machine Gun Squadron transferred by to D.A.D.O.S. 2nd Division. Carriage Ord Q.F. 18 pdr No 28264 of B/210 Bde R.F.A. condemned for wear.	FS
—	25-6-18		Ord Q.F. 18 pdr No 321 of B/211 Bde R.F.A. condemned for wear	FS
—	26-6-18		4.5" Howitzer No 163 and carriage No 2403b condemned destroyed by shell fire	FS

WAR DIARY
INTELLIGENCE SUMMARY

Army Form C.2118.

Sheet 4

Place	Date	Hour	Summary of Events and Information	Remarks and references to Appendices
HQ/52-1st Bde / Bustindon	2/6/18		Rct. Off. up for no 1639 and Gunner no 99265 of B/210 Bde RFA condemned to Penal Servitude	F.9
			50 fuses nose large rounds to 42nd Divisional Train for trial and report. 50 Ringer Bombardier shots issued { 10 to each Inf Bde, 10 to 3rd & 10th A Bns }	F.9
			Pte QM Sjt. Upon Co. Hoy. of B/210 Bde RFA condemned serving unless Staff Sergt. of Rank	F.9

SECRET. Vol 18

War Diary

of

D.A.D.O.S. 42nd Division

July 1918.

Army Form C. 2118.

WAR DIARY
of
INTELLIGENCE SUMMARY.
(Erase heading not required.)

1st Sheet

Instructions regarding War Diaries and Intelligence Summaries are contained in F. S. Regs., Part II. and the Staff Manual respectively. Title pages will be prepared in manuscript.

Place	Date	Hour	Summary of Events and Information	Remarks and references to Appendices
Bnor-b-Outre	1-4-18	—	Ord QF 18pdr No 528 of B/311 Bde RFA condemned scoring. Replaced by No 9328	J.T.S.
—	4-4-18	—	Ord 4.5" Howitzer No 1932 and carriage with all sights (No 13145) of B/311 Bde RFA condemned premature. Replaced by New No 3032 and carriage No 134A5.	J.T.S.
—	8-4-18		Offices and Dump moved with Rear Divisional Headquarters to Tarton.	J.T.S.
Tarton	9-4-18		30 Lewis Guns issued to complete all Infantry Battalions to scale 'G'.	J.T.S.
—	10-4-18		Lnt Frontingo HA (Lewis Gun Monkey Rifle Type) issued to 125 Infantry Bde. Visited SOS No 28 Workshop to enquire into the matter of Ord QF 18pdr No 3969 reported by RFA because of inaccurate shooting. Called on ADOS IIIth Corps with reference to issue of trench inventions for Pickwer Guns. Inspected Quartermasters Stores of 1/4 Northumberland (Pioneers) and 42 M.G. Bn.	J.T.S.
—	11-4-18		Ord QF 18pdr No 1350 of B/310 Bde RFA and Ord QF 18pdr No 5514 of B/310 Bde RFA both condemned scoring, replaced by No 1089 and 5709. Visited 1/8 L and 1/2 H Field Ambulances with reference to the de-gassing of LD clothing.	J.T.S.
—	12-4-18		Inspected Quartermaster's Dumps of 1/5th, 1/6th and 1/7th Manchester Regts. Visited baths at Louvencourt, and arranged for men's bathing parade, also	J.T.S.

Army Form C. 2118.

WAR DIARY
INTELLIGENCE SUMMARY.
(Erase heading not required.)

2nd Sheet

Place	Date	Hour	Summary of Events and Information	Remarks and references to Appendices
Sailly	12-4-18	—	Ord. H.S. Howitzer No 2633 and carriage No. 8499, withdrawn, all night, of D/210 Bde R.F.A. condemned for Remation.	J.9
—	13-4-18	—	Limber mounting for Vickers Gun drawn from 3rd Heavy Mobile workshop, and issued to L.R.E. at Bertrancourt.	J.9
—	14-4-18	—	Visited 19th Mobile Vet Section and 1/10 Manchester Regt.	J.9
—	15-4-18	—	Inspected Stores and dump of D.A.D.O.S. 54th Division at Authie, with a view to taking over same. Visited Staff Captain 124 Infantry Bde, also 1/1st and 1/2nd of Field Ambulance and advanced D.H.Q.	J.9
—	16-4-18	—	Reference Office and Dump moved to Authie. Inspected Soldier Kitns and Salvage Dumps at Bus and Beaucourt. Visited A.R.Ps and discussed return of empties by D.A.C. Wagons, these being empties for Dunnage, and other points of economy.	J.9
Authie	18-4-18	—	Visited D.A.D.O.S. IV Corps. Inspected Salvage Dumps and re-arranged Personnel to augment the output of Solder. 9 men from Viscount Kerr.	J.9

Army Form C. 2118.

WAR DIARY
INTELLIGENCE SUMMARY.
(Erase heading not required.)

3rd Sheet

Place	Date	Hour	Summary of Events and Information	Remarks and references to Appendices
Authie	19.4.18	—	Damaged QF 18 Pdr No 54883 of B/210 Bde RFA condemned for wear replaced by No 58. Visited 196 Bde RA regarding proposed method of carriage of Lewis Guns. Also discussed the system of cleaning and delivering of Lewis Breas clothing. Afterwards visited 15/17th Hrs and 1/10 Manchester Regt.	F.S.
—	22.4.18	—	Visited SOS No 98 workshops regarding repairs to water carts. Lewis Breas clothing drawn from OC IV Army Troops No4 in accordance with third Army Instructions.	F.S.
—	24.4.18	—	Visited OC MT Coy and arranged periodical inspection of Hotchkiss Guns, also Hotchkiss Guns of 3rd Train and Lewis Guns of Batteries, Field Companies and RAC.	F.S.
—	25.4.18	—	Ord. QF 18 pdr. No 3494 of B/210 Bde RFA. condemned as inaccurate, authority Q.M.G. 5055 (S.C.) dated 2.1.18. Visited SAA section RAC regarding care of Lewis Guns on charge. Inspected Lewis Guns and storage Pumps no Bus and Javencourt. Also on OC 3rd Echn 3rd Train, and examined all ordnance belonging incidents with him, found everything satisfactory. Inspected Gun dumps of 1st and No 2 Section RAC, and disclosed each of authorised spare parts	F.S.

Army Form C. 2118.

WAR DIARY
or
INTELLIGENCE SUMMARY.   4th Sheet
(Erase heading not required.)

Instructions regarding War Diaries and Intelligence Summaries are contained in F.S. Regs., Part II. and the Staff Manual respectively. Title pages will be prepared in manuscript.

Place	Date	Hour	Summary of Events and Information	Remarks and references to Appendices
Aukra	26-4-16	—	Ord. QF 18 pdr 710 & 185 of B/210 Bde RFA examined scoring. All outstanding indents reviewed. Four Hotchkiss guns of Divisional Train inspected by Armourer, who reported all in excellent condition.	F.J.
—	27-4-16	—	Inspected A.R.P. with A.901 Tk Corps, and arranged for the supply of fire extinguishers, also the lending of a Corrugated Iron Shed for the storing of 45" mountain cartridges. Called on 186 Bde Hqrs and inspection allowance sheet for LD clothing.	F.J.
—	28-4-16	—	Visited 28 and 45 DT.M.W.(Trench) regarding Carts, Water, Tank G.S. 136 Bde. Inspected A.R.P., also called on OC MT Coy. A/Armas + Clerk left for temporary duty with 80th Division, A.E.F.	F.J.
—	30-4-16	—	Visited 136 & Farm Field Ambulance regarding issue of tables and forms. Inspected Soldier Riders of Bus and farm transport.	F.J.
—	3-4-16	—	Visited 2/B 210 Bde RFA and interviewed O.C. Two thousand hundred blankets drawn from O.O.II Corps Troops to be held by A.D.O.S. as a reserve	F.J.

Secret

Vol 19

D.A.D.O.S.
-9 SEP 1918
42ND (E. LANCS.) DIV.

War Diary

of

D.A.D.O.S. 42nd. Division

Army Form C. 2118.

WAR DIARY
or
INTELLIGENCE SUMMARY.
(Erase heading not required.)

Instructions regarding War Diaries and Intelligence Summaries are contained in F. S. Regs., Part II. and the Staff Manual respectively. Title pages will be prepared in manuscript.

1st Sheet

Place	Date	Hour	Summary of Events and Information	Remarks and references to Appendices
Authie	3-8-18		Inspected Salvage Dumps at Bus & Louvencourt. Old 4.5" How 244 of 9/20 Bde RFA condemned through wear replaced by 2643	F.9.
—	4-8-18		Visited S.A. Dot H.Q Division. Interviewed OC No 2 Cy Divisional Train, also OPM Section DAC. Inspected dozen boxes of 3" Lighter Mortar with Albion fuzes	F.9.
—	5-8-18		Visited 125 Bde returned Mks with DA gages. Inspected rear dump at Doullens Old RF Hows No 4431 of B/20 Bde RFA condemned for scoring, replaced by 11182	F.9.
—	6-8-18		Visited Railhead and watched unloading and checking of stores on to lorries. Visited 66 Bde Advanced Headquarters, and 10th SAMC, interviewed Staff Captain with reference to outstanding stores. Inspected Baths at Couples.	F.9.
—	8-8-18		Visited No 28 OM Workshop (right) also Corps Salvage Dumps. New site for Solder Kiln selected at Louvencourt.	F.9.
—	9-8-18		Arranged for all Bottles at Salvage Dump to be sent to Orville. Visited 124 Bde Refilling Point and watched issue of stores. Inspected A.R.P.	F.9.
—	10-8-18		Carriage 18 pdr No 30434 of B/20 Bde RFA condemned damaged, replaced by 11203.	F.9.

Army Form C. 2118.

WAR DIARY
or
INTELLIGENCE SUMMARY.
(Erase heading not required.)

2nd Sheet

Instructions regarding War Diaries and Intelligence Summaries are contained in F. S. Regs., Part II. and the Staff Manual respectively. Title pages will be prepared in manuscript.

Place	Date	Hour	Summary of Events and Information	Remarks and references to Appendices
Authie	14-8-18		Lewis Guns tested on Range. Visited BABDI Hg Division at Gorun.	FJ
	12-8-18		Visited Conference of BABDI with BDO° Third Army and ADO° Fourth Corps at Labusse Ammunition Railhead. Inspected 31st and 32nd A.R.D.	FJ
	13-8-18		Vanda movement depot with RA & DMG also rear dumps of Divisional Signal School, Divisional Reception Camps and Lewis Guns School. Return forwarded to ADO° of issues demanded on Base for month of June and July. Inspected A.R.D.	FJ
	14-8-18			FJ
	15-8-18		Officer and dump moved to New Location, billeted in School-room. Temporary method of carrying completed at O.f.E.	FJ
Bus-les-Artois	16-8-18		Inspected Lewis Guns, and wagon equipment of No 2 Coy 43rd Div. train. Visited Salvage Dumps and inspected salved shells with Corps Ammunition Officer, noted unexploded shells dangerous, and made arrangements to destroy.	FJ
	17-8-18		Visited DE Divisional HQrs and interviewed Staff Captain. Also interviewed Brigade Major and Adjutant of 211 R.H. RFA at their HQ No 6 Coy BDe of C/90 Bde RFA (No 3 Subs.) condemned for corvey replaced by No 2000	FJ

Army Form C. 2118.

WAR DIARY
of
INTELLIGENCE SUMMARY.
(Erase heading not required.)

3rd Sheet

Place	Date	Hour	Summary of Events and Information	Remarks and references to Appendices
Bng-be-Ubaq	16-8-18		Visited Bde Transport lines with BAQMG and inspected QM dumps, shoemakers shops, also tailors shops of the three Infantry Battalions. Found all working satisfactorily.	878
	18-8-18		Visited Railhead and Corps Salvage Dumps. Interviewed all M.T. Coy and reviewed outstanding indents.	878
			Ord. Q= 18/par No 6914 of a/210 Bde RFA condemned for chamber scoring, replaced by No 9345.	878
	20-8-18		Pack Saddles and Water Carriers issued to all Brigades, also 400 extra water-bottles and 100 Wire-cutters	878
			80 rifles and 80 complete SAA equipment sent to Bde Reserve	878
	22-8-18		Ord 4.5 How No 2310 with barrage No 2643 of A/210 Bde RFA condemned for premature, replaced by No 6-3	878
			Ord Q= 18/par No 9382 of 18/210 Bde RFA condemned for scoring, replaced by No 30 H.O.	878
	23-8-18		Ord Q.F 18/pdr No 5820 of 13/211 Bde RFA condemned for inaccuracy, authority QMG 8055 of 31/7/18. History sheet to Gun Park, replaced by No 60	878
	23-8-18		Ord 4.5 How No 2790 and barrage No 2403g condemned for premature, replaced by Sgt 3130 and 13197.	878

Army Form C. 2118.

WAR DIARY
or
INTELLIGENCE SUMMARY.
(Erase heading not required.)

Instructions regarding War Diaries and Intelligence Summaries are contained in F. S. Regs., Part II. and the Staff Manual respectively. Title pages will be prepared in manuscript.

4th Sheet

Place	Date	Hour	Summary of Events and Information	Remarks and references to Appendices
Bus. les Artois	22-8-18		Ord QF 18 pdr No 9283 of B/310 Bde RFA, condemned shell fire, replaced by No 1614.	878
			Carriage QF 18 pdr No 12363 of B/310 Bde RFA condemned for wear, replaced by 5924	878
	24-8-18		Works 6th & 28 D.I workshop 2 & 6 Engineers repairing "bearing of gun from Gun Park at workshops by lorries	878
			R.H.Q moved to Bienvillers.	878
	25-8-18		Railhead moved to Beaumetz	
			Ord QF 18 pdr No 11045 Hows and carriage No 51 of A/211 Bde RFA condemned through premature, replaced by Nos 1105 and 1431.	878
			Ord QF 18.P.A. No 864 condemned wearing and carriage QF 18 pdr No 10540 condemned shell fire (B/310 Bde RFA) replaced by 1015 and 15 B4B.	878
	26-8-18		Used B/HQ as Divisional Amm. Column, RPA.	878
	27-8-18		Moved BHQ	878
	28-8-18		BHQ moved to Burgues.	878
	29-8-18		Ord QF 18 pdr No 6448 of B/310 Bde RFA condemned for scoring, replaced by 9553.	879
			Ord QF 18 pdr No 4566 of B/311 Bde RFA condemned for scoring, replaced by 9760	879

A 5834 Wt. W4973/M687 750,000 8/16 D. D. & L. Ltd. Forms/C.2118/13.

Army Form C. 2118.

WAR DIARY
INTELLIGENCE SUMMARY.   5th Sheet
(Erase heading not required.)

Place	Date	Hour	Summary of Events and Information	Remarks and references to Appendices
Monument	30-8-18		Railroad moved to Monument. Forward dump moved to Monument, leaving stores at Gure-les-Artois u/a of or A.D and D.Sum.	F.9
Py8	31-8-18		Moved forward dump to Py8. A.R.Q.M.G. carried on equipping baths with washing, dryers, gloves etc.	F.9

WR 20

War Diary
September, 1918
D.A.D.O.S. 42nd Divn.

SECRET

WAR DIARY
or
INTELLIGENCE SUMMARY.

Army Form C. 2118.

(Erase heading not required.)

Place	Date	Hour	Summary of Events and Information	Remarks and references to Appendices
Pup	2.9.18		Visited Wl.Qn. at Grevillers. Cleared dumps at Puis & Irougts forward remainder of men's stores to Pup.	JS
"	3.9.18		Reinculation of 63rd Division attached for administration of 42nd Div. only. Captured Machine Guns & Mortars pubs on rail at Miraumont. Total of captured guns sent to rail to dump 189. Trench mortars 11.	JS
"	4.9.18		D.H.Q. moves to Puisieux.	JS
"	5.9.18		Railhead moved to Achiet-le-Grand. Division coming out to refit. Collected 200 tents from Miraumont sent to units. Looting officer attached for collection of all enemy guns and mortars.	JS
"	6.9.18		Division sent out of the line. Visited D.H.Q. and new D.A.Q.M.G. & S.C.R.A. at 45" R.A. authorised to retain 80 rds of Packsaddlery to be handed over to Corps troops refpo. Issued 200 tents to units. Notified Corps Camp and Rouen that Division were out of line.	JS
"	7.9.18		Cleared 58 tents from Town Major Auchie. Visited 30 to 127 Field Visited D.H.Q, also Baths at Warlencourt. Wired for Clothing & Boots.	JS
"	8.9.18		Called at Corps W.l.Qn. and interviewed A.D.O.S. Visited D.H.Q. Military Des. Pups to trucks out from Town & 1 Rouen also 5 mitrailleur.	JS

Army Form C. 2118.

WAR DIARY
or
INTELLIGENCE SUMMARY. Second Sheet
(Erase heading not required.)

Instructions regarding War Diaries and Intelligence
Summaries are contained in F. S. Regs., Part II.
and the Staff Manual respectively. Title pages
will be prepared in manuscript.

Place	Date	Hour	Summary of Events and Information	Remarks and references to Appendices
Pays	9.9.18		Visited following units with Staff Capt: 1/7 Bde.: 1/9 Bn 127, 1/5, 1/6 1/7 Manchesters, 50" & 51" Bn's and Quartermasters. No complaints. Also visited 2 Corps Main, 127 to T.M.B., 127 Field Coy.	F.S.
	10.9.18		Visited Staff Captains 42 & 6" Div. Antys. Sent clean clothing & forwarded dumps. Also 1/127 D.A.C. A.A.Q.M.G. called re comparative statements of clothing etc.	F.S.
	11.9.18		Inspected all new Brigade dumps with respective Staff Captains. All stores sorted into three categories. A.D.O.S. called.	F.S.
	12.9.18		Visited N.D.O.S. re ?? rifles magazines and Lewis gun chests now this battalion. Sent 30 guns going into action only 20 magazines sent re issued. Visited D.H.Q. re battalion dumps as Bus.	F.S.
	14.9.18		A.D.O.S called	F.S.
	15.9.18		Bus to Radincourt met Salvage officer and took particulars of 11 Lewis guns. Visited D.H.Q. & saw A.D.M.S. took motor despatched by 1/4 Manchesters. Inspecting Dressing Varely. Issued.	F.S.
	16.9.18		Visited D.H.Q. with Staff Cart 125 Bde. Inspected ammunition dump of 1/7 Manchesters & found everything O.K.	F.S.

Army Form C. 2118.

WAR DIARY
or
INTELLIGENCE SUMMARY. Thumbnail
(Erase heading not required.)

Instructions regarding War Diaries and Intelligence Summaries are contained in F. S. Regs., Part II. and the Staff Manual respectively. Title pages will be prepared in manuscript.

Place	Date	Hour	Summary of Events and Information	Remarks and references to Appendices
H.Q.	17.9.18		Inspected B.M. stores of 117 F/B from Tournette Staff Capatain. Capt. Newby proceeded to France. Relief went for.	J.S.
	18.9.18		Visited D.A.D. O.S. 97 Div. at Lebuquier with a view to take over on the 21st. Called at D.H.Q.	J.S.
	19.9.18		" and saw D.A.Q.M.G. and S.b.A.A. regarding issue of fur Rugs.	J.S.
	20.4.18		Demanded fur Rugs etc.	J.S.
	21.4.18		Moved to LEBUCQUIERE and took over office and dump from 97th Division.	J.S.
Lebucquiere	22.9.18		Visited Corps M.N. Gen. and had interviews with A.D.O.S. Arranged inspection of Dial Ships by Inspector in accordance with S.G.R.O. 4517.	J.S.
			Divisional Rail. M.T. Coy Inspecting issue of Clothing. R.n.S. thoroughly into the matter sent to D.B. and Adjt. Q.M.S.	J.S.
	23.9.18		Issued 8 Rifles, 5 pairs of Inspections to Reception Camp. A.A.Q.M.G. called to Reft Camps & Bath Works. 300 lbs of Soap on demand & 1500 Disks. Lost in stock.	J.S.
	24.4.18		Cpl. Atkinson of D.ADMT. completed his week's course on Lewis Gun. Inspector of Shops reported to me. Programme of inspection arranged with Staff Captains.	J.S.
	25.9.18		Inspected Shoemakers shops with Inspector & found everything satisfactory.	J.S.

Army Form C. 2118.

WAR DIARY
or
INTELLIGENCE SUMMARY.
(Erase heading not required.)

Instructions regarding War Diaries and Intelligence Summaries are contained in F. S. Regs., Part II. and the Staff Manual respectively. Title pages will be prepared in manuscript.

Place	Date	Hour	Summary of Events and Information	Remarks and references to Appendices
Lihons	25.9.18		Collected 200 Petrol tins for Medical Purpose	FS
"	26.9.18		Called at Gun Park for Rifle exchange vouchers. Had interview with A.D.O.S. Called at Main dressing Station & saw Ole. Demanded fresh return	FS
"	27.9.18		Dined D.H.Q. Issued tents to 3rd Hussars. Heard new outbreak of blankets & horses rugs units being on the move	FS
"	28.9.18		Railhead changed to YTRES. A.A.&Q.M.G. called & discussed issue of winter clothing	FS
"	29.9.18		Dined D.H.Q. and arranged rifling Truck for artillery. Had interview with Brig Gen. I.A. re issue of guns. 150 blankets arrived	FS

SECRET.

No 21

WAR DIARY — OCTOBER, 1918.

D.A.D.O.S. 42ND DIVISION.

Army Form C. 2118.

WAR DIARY
INTELLIGENCE SUMMARY.
(Erase heading not required.)

First sheet

Place	Date	Hour	Summary of Events and Information	Remarks and references to Appendices
Aurgembourg	2.10.16		Moved stamp and offices to Aurgembourg. Direct Road for nofs roap for French fees destines	F19
	3.10.16		Granted leave to U.K. Col. Downing left in charge.	F19
	4.10.16		Visited Neuilhead and I.O.M. A.A.'Q.M.G called. No complaints	F19
	5.10.16		Ol Suffolk Col called re shipments of M.T. men attacked. Decided to continue shipping them as before. Visited I.O.M. re water carts for 61,2.10 which arrived from Rouen with wrong petrol role. Also visited A.D.O.S. Ty roops and obtained truth. Received notification to demand Drivers uniform and tests also F.9. Roofs supplied to A.D.O.S. Thus F.9. Roots should now be issued until such boots in use had become unserviceable.	F19
			D.A.Q.M.G called. Heaps return attached. Props to be made immediately	F19
	6.11.16		A.A.'S.Q.M.G called and instructed me to issue each Infantry Br. with 500 uniform. Jur roops to be issued to complete. D.A.A.G called re Rents. Received 1500 roops	F19
	7.11.16		A.D.O.S called and infected stamps, everything O.K. Received 1500 roops of various from Gun Parts to issue for contain regarding each mfr role to avail 600 roops.	F19

Army Form C. 2118.

WAR DIARY
or
INTELLIGENCE SUMMARY. Second sheet.
(Erase heading not required.)

Instructions regarding War Diaries and Intelligence Summaries are contained in F. S. Regs., Part II. and the Staff Manual respectively. Title pages will be prepared in manuscript.

Place	Date	Hour	Summary of Events and Information	Remarks and references to Appendices
Auxi le Chateau	9.10.18		Visited A. & Q.M.G at Corbie with reference to moving dumps	JS
EGNES	10.10.18		Moved Offices and stores to hurra. 2 Days Philip Coat granted leave to U.K.	JS
—	11.10.18		Visited A.A.&Q.M.G re winter clothing. Decided to submit demands and arch rue to hold until Div. are in a position to accept. Pte Clough 739 Dumps Coy. granted leave to U.K. In future stores to be sent to Neuflin, Paris	JS
—	12.10.18		Northern moved to Longeaucourt from YPRES.	JS
—	13.10.18		Visited officer clothing depots as demands rising to return payment notes. Called on Q.O. Corps nothwo. M.T. Coy re return to cars, and I.O.M.	JS
BEAUVOIS	14.10.18		Moved offices and stores to Beauvois. Move completed on 15th inst.	JS
—	15.10.18		Visited A.A.&Q.M.G all Four Employment Comes attached by Div. to move reception camps. Demanded all winter clothing and asked Rue not to issue until units can accept.	JS
—	16.10.18		Goes car to Bethrhops for repair. Spoke to "Q" actions moving 103 D.O. Coy. Nothing definite about moving at present. A.D.O.S called and inspected dumps. No complaints.	JS

A.5834 Wt. W4973/M687 750,000 8/16 D. D. & L. Ltd. Forms/C.2118/13.

WAR DIARY / INTELLIGENCE SUMMARY

Army Form C. 2118.

Place: **PROVEN** — Vischeer (?)

Date	Hour	Summary of Events and Information	Remarks
17.10.16		A. & Q.M.G. called re Tarpaulins. District Reception Camps re issue of clothing.	afs
18.10.16		D.A.D.O.S. reorganised and 37th Divn. called. The latter has a surplus of Boots and will notify later how many he can spare. A.D.O.S. called.	afs
19.10.16		Returned from leave	afs
20.10.16		A. & Q.M.G. instructed me to meet Rev. Thos. Rio our accredited winter clothing. Called on A.D.O.S. also called on I.O.M. regarding 18th. M.D. 4106 and Transport which was destroyed by incendiary belonging to D/410	afs
21.10.16		Inspected Divl. dumps ELESNES and D.A.Q.M.G. Called on 120 & 127 Inf. Bde. Bns and had interview with Brigadier. Arranged that woollen drawers complaints should be sent through Bde.	afs
22.10.16		Motor Lorries tipped for four S. Camps moved. 12,000 veils moved to clean clothing stores.	afs
23.10.16		Visited to 110 M.A. Cov. and had interview with A.D.O.S. re winter underclothing being issued to clean clothing store. Inspected Divl. Salvage dumps met D.A.Q.M.G.	afs
24.10.16		Divl. O.C. 1/3 East Divn. 127 Bns/S. T.M.B. and 1/2 Fd. Ambulance	afs
25.10.16		Divl. Staff Captains 125 and 127 Brigades and discussed refitting of Brigades and Battalions Lewis Guns equipments	afs

WAR DIARY
INTELLIGENCE SUMMARY

Army Form C. 2118.

(Erase heading not required.)

Instructions regarding War Diaries and Intelligence Summaries are contained in F.S. Regs., Part II. and the Staff Manual respectively. Title pages will be prepared in manuscript.

Rough notes

Place	Date	Hour	Summary of Events and Information	Remarks and references to Appendices
BEADNOIS	25.10.16		Also discussed with Staff Captain 12 S.& 127 Div. the "Stationing" of certain items of clothing and Equipments as per G.R.O. 1773.	FJS
—	26.10.16		Sent to Doullens with D.A.Q.M.G. to enquire amount of Garment returns on Ind. dumps there. Attended a conference during the morning helped on to Doullens of all Commander's officers Scrounge. in command Staff Captains and A.A. & Q.M.G. regarding reception in rear of Divn gun experiments Salvage dumps and other matters.	FJS
—	28.10.16		Returned from Doullens with D.A.Q.M.G. Arranged refilling points for Divl. Artillery.	FJS
—	29.10.16		Transferred 23rd Divl. Arty. to 63rd Divn. Divisn Amm. Pn. Cav. to see A.D.O.S. two lorry loads of stores sent to Arty. refilling point.	FJS
—	30.10.16		Visited Div. Arr. station at Toutencourt with D.A.Q.M.G. called on N.A.Cavalry and inspected R.M. new huttings. in good order. Received a fresh load of winter clothing, F.S. Boots, woollen gloves etc.	FJS
—	31.10.16		Visited New Zealand Div. as Gokormer with D.A.Q.M.G. Called at Artillery refilling dumps and inspected issue of stores to units. Visited I.O.M. No 25, 46 workshops and arranged with him about the building of Ditchers from nippers with steel bunkers in Gun Pk. armourer and an artificer Sm. J.	FJS

WD 22

War Diary
D.A.D.O.S. 42nd Division

November

SECRET.

WAR DIARY
INTELLIGENCE SUMMARY.

Army Form C. 2118.

Place	Date	Hour	Summary of Events and Information	Remarks and references to Appendices
BEAUVOIS	1-11-18		Artillery lorries sent to refilling points. Sent chief clerk to all salvage and Div. Ordnance dumps in Corps area to collect all available Stokes supporting for use with Pancho Magazine items gun. Cleared two dumps of Lewis gun stores from Cavalry Railhead that had been forwarded from Div. dumps at Doullens.	719
-do-	2-11-18		A.A. & Q.M.G. inquired if 4th Army hand or Stokes till per infty. Bn. could be obtained for a special purpose. Ascertained from A.D.O.S. IV Corps that the C.E. Army was arranging for issue of these items from R.E. Parks on a scale of 400 per Div. Arms moved to complete units to establishments of all Lewis gun equipments (magazine, Pouches, Cosmos melt, etc.) Returned 9 unserviceable civil rights to Heavy mobile Workshops. Called on No.3 officers clothing depot.	718 / 718
-do-	3-11-18		Railhead moved to Cambrai. Armure temporarily transferred with A.O.O. there to hand out all vehicles accruing to respective units. Visited Div HQ 4th Arm.	718 / 718
-do-	4-11-18		Visited A.D.O.S. IV Corps. Inspected Salvage dumps at Aulencourt Ferme and found everything satisfactory. Suspended issue of stores on hand.	718

Ref. Porven.

Army Form C. 2118.

WAR DIARY
INTELLIGENCE SUMMARY.

(Erase heading not required.)

Instructions regarding War Diaries and Intelligence Summaries are contained in F. S. Regs., Part II. and the Staff Manual respectively. Title pages will be prepared in manuscript.

Place	Date	Hour	Summary of Events and Information	Remarks and references to Appendices
BEAUVOIS	5.11.16		Div. H.Q. moved to Beaudignies	FS
LE GUESNOY	6.11.16		Issued offers to Bureaus and part of stores, and shops to be brought forward as early as possible	FS
	8.11.16		Called at Div. H.Q.'s at Potelle Chateau and arranged with "Q" to deliver 1000 prs of socks and clean washing from Clothing store at Maurois to advanced dumps at Neuvilgnies. A.D.O.S. IV Corps called and informed me that Pack artillery would be used as required unless arrangements made by Corps.	FS
	9.11.16		Visited 1/4 Fd. Ambulance at Marion Range with a view to taking over billets and stores occupied by them for use as dump for officers	FS
			Called at Div. H.Q. and interviewed with D.A.Q.M.G. to collect Sock numbers and for use as Panniers and journey to Neuvilgnies	FS
	10.11.16		Double Maurois Range went advanced with OC 1/4 Fd. Ambce to take over	FS
Marion Range	11.11.16		Issued Officers Mess in Lorry length of place to Maurois Range	FS
	12.11.16		Visited Div. H.Q. and interviewed with A.A.S.Q.M.G. regarding move of Corps Troops and of ways & sources. Situation as good in this respect all ranks with one or two	FS

Army Form C. 2118.

WAR DIARY
INTELLIGENCE SUMMARY.   3rd Sheet.
(Erase heading not required.)

Place	Date	Hour	Summary of Events and Information	Remarks and references to Appendices
Mouen Rouge	14/11/16		Called on O.C. H.Q. M.T. Coy and arranged to return three of my lorries to Column. Their lorries to remain with column to clear Ordnance stores while Railhead is so far in rear of Div. O.C. M.T. Coy to supply extra lorries if required.	JFS
— —	15/11/16		Directed refilling points at Neuvenmont. Sent two lorries for clubs with Column. Must down to be sent later. Rail head not attached to M.T. Coy to convey Ordnance stores from Railhead to my dump. Directed Div. Vet. Ons. as to unloading and arranged to move office and dump there. Discussed return of all special stores to Base work Q.	JFS
Hautmesnil	16/11/16		Moved office and dumps to Hautmesnil. M.T. Coy supplied six lorries for this work. Directed base shipping docks and found more machine essential. Demanded shipper on loan & by wire for same who had not already indented for same.	JFS
— —	17/11/16		As announced refitting Div. for forward mvmt. Travel home things to Chippen's Centre.	JFS
— —	18/11/16		11:00 Blankets arrived at Railhead for mine of second Klavrht.	JFS
— —	19/11/16		Held at Railhead laundry and arranged to clear blankets to Outhouse Farm Reception camp. Started the night at Reception camp. M.T. Coy supplied six lorries for this work. Returning to Hautmesnil following morning.	JFS

WAR DIARY

INTELLIGENCE SUMMARY.
(Erase heading not required.)

Army Form C. 2118.

Instructions regarding War Diaries and Intelligence Summaries are contained in F. S. Regs., Part II. and the Staff Manual respectively. Title pages will be prepared in manuscript.

4th Sheet

Place	Date	Hour	Summary of Events and Information	Remarks and references to Appendices
Montbrehain	20-11-18		Interviewed Quarter Master at Aubiencourt Farm who new nothing our stores for this respective units as Div. dumps there. Called on O.C. D.O.S. at Rugny regarding disposal of 100 tents handed in by units to my dump at Montbrehain.	GFS
" "	21-11-18		Inspected dumps of surplus stores returned by units to Factory Montbrehain and notified "Q" that four lorries would clear M.T. Coy. instructed to place stores at my disposal for this month to remove to Roullant.	GFS
" "	22-11-18		Visited 127 Fd. Mt. Coy. and discussed the "Rationing" of Clothing with O.C. Found the old N.C.O. proceeded to Aubiencourt Farm to take over surplus Ordnance stores as Divl. dump and return same to Rave. Checked all contents in view of approaching "Reclaments"	GFS
" "	23-11-18			GFS
" "	24-11-18		O.C. to Monchester called at my office to inquire what stores could be retained Informed him that all special stores not included as part of units equipment on Mob. Q. car table should be returned to our ford depositch to Rave.	GFS
" "	25-11-18		Inspected all transport of the Field Artillery hm of 125 Bde.	GFS
" "	26-11-18		Received 2 Stuart Leather machines, 20 tops 20 bottom plates and 500 spare parts for my Stuart	GFS

Army Form C. 2118.

WAR DIARY
INTELLIGENCE SUMMARY. 5th sheet.
(Erase heading not required.)

Instructions regarding War Diaries and Intelligence Summaries are contained in F. S. Regs., Part II. and the Staff Manual respectively. Title pages will be prepared in manuscript.

Place	Date	Hour	Summary of Events and Information	Remarks and references to Appendices
Heudicourt	27.11.16		Visited No. 1/1c Manchesters and inspected Q. M. Stores.	JFS
— " —	28.11.16		Motored to Tincourt and called on D.A.D.O.S. 37th Div. to collect seven stewart supply machines for use in Div. Clipping centre. Called on A.A. & Q.M.G. V Corps re proposed attempt to collect 500 blankets from his dumps. This number will complete Div. with issue of second blanket.	JFS
— " —	29.11.16		Inspected Salved Ammunition dumps at Marquies with D.A.Q.M.G. Estimated quantity valued to be about 125 lorry loads. Visited D/210 A.W R.F.A. to inspect vehicles, and stores damaged by explosion.	JFS

SECRET

Vol. 23

War Diary
of
D.A.D.O.S. 42 Division
December 1918.

Army Form C. 2118.

WAR DIARY
~~INTELLIGENCE SUMMARY.~~

Sheet 1

(Erase heading not required.)

Instructions regarding War Diaries and Intelligence Summaries are contained in F. S. Regs., Part II. and the Staff Manual respectively. Title pages will be prepared in manuscript.

Place	Date	Hour	Summary of Events and Information	Remarks and references to Appendices
Haulmont	2-12-18		Visited Charleroi to inspect new area regarding accommodation.	AFB
—	6-12-18		Inspected Workshops Depot of animals supposed or not. Machines being repaired by British Personnel, equipment in good order.	AFB
—	8-12-18		Visited RTO Le Quesnoy to arrange for reconsignment of trucks to new area.	AFB
—	7-12-18		Inspected Transport of 104 Infantry Bde at Haulmont.	AFB
—	8-12-18		Inspected Divisional Baths, no complaints as regards supply of clean clothing.	AFB
—			HQ. A.B.C Batteries, Ammn Column of 93. A.F.A Bde transferred from 60 Fd Coys Troops for Ordnance Administration. Ammn Dump. Rank Relief Clerk evacuated sick to B.E.F	AFB
—	10-12-18			AFB
—	13-12-18		Interviewed A.D.S. and reference to supply of palliasses. 300 required urgently.	AFB
Charleroi	14-12-18		Office and Store established at Charleroi.	AFB
—	17-12-18		A.A.+Q.M.G. called reference palliasses and latrine Buckets for Barracks Charleroi	AFB

A.5834 Wt. W4973/M687 750,000 8/16 D. D. & L. Ltd. Forms/C.2118/13.

Army Form C.2118.

WAR DIARY
or
INTELLIGENCE SUMMARY. 2nd Sheet

(Erase heading not required.)

Place	Date	Hour	Summary of Events and Information	Remarks and references to Appendices
Calais	16-12-18		Visited HQ 93 AFA Bde, and interviewed with OC. Arranged loan of Horse Clipping Machine.	STS
—	17-12-18		Visited 2OO Frontigny, and interviewed RTO with reference to delay of trucks due from Calais. Was interviewed Staff Captain RA	STS
—	20-12-18		Called at Bay Bde HQ at Fleurus, and interviewed OC and Staff Captain. Arrangements made to send all Ordnance stores to refilling point at Town Hall, Fleurus.	STS
—	21-12-18		First three truck loads of stores arrived from Calais. Called at HQr Divisional train.	STS
—	24-12-18		Visited Machine Gun Bn at Velaine inspection QM stores. Indents submitted to Base for 3rd Blankets.	STS

SECRET

Vol 24

War Diary for the month of January, 1919

D.A.D.O.S. 42nd Division

Army Form C. 2118.

WAR DIARY
INTELLIGENCE SUMMARY

January 1919 Sheet 1

Place	Date	Hour	Summary of Events and Information	Remarks and references to Appendices
Chodeau	7-1-19		No. 34 Labour Coy, 59th & 94th Labour Companies, Fourth Army Medical School, Fourth Army Air Veterinary Hospital, attached to me for Ordnance administration.	GN
—	8-1-19		No. 15 Ordnance Mobile Workshop (Light) transferred from OD 4th Army Troops No 2 to me for Ordnance service. Lance Ll Hardy RAOC reported as Chief Clerk.	GN
—	10-1-19		Visited Nos 28 & 145 OMW (Light) at Lembour with reference to repairs for Divisional Artillery. Also called on OC 48 Divl Reception Camp, and OC IVth Corps Concentration Camp. No. 5 Ord. Mobile Workshop (Heavy) transferred from OC 4th Army Troops No 2 to me for Ordnance Administration.	GN
—	11-1-19		The undermentioned stores (German) taken over from B.R.E. Fourth Army. By orders of DADS for issue as required. Brushes Scrubbing 730 " Sweeping 150 Paillasses 3900 Lamps Oil 145 " Carbide 115	GN

Army Form C. 2118.

WAR DIARY

INTELLIGENCE SUMMARY.
(Erase heading not required.)

Sheet 2

Place	Date	Hour	Summary of Events and Information	Remarks and references to Appendices
Charleroi.	12-1-19.		332. Road Construction Coy. transferred to me by OC 13th Corps Tps for Ordnance Ammunition. 59th Sanitary Section arrived from 46th Division, and attached for Ordnance Stores	GF.
—	13-1-19		Officers and Dump moved to No 3 Rue des Rivages, Charleroi. Wanted A.297 Corps reference stores for Concentration Camp	GF
—	16-1-19		Three O.R. Q.F. 18 pdr. limbered wagons received for 13/93 A.F.A. Bde.	GF
—	19-1-19		Bicycles, Bags Armourer Bicycle (pedal), Sadding Officers tendered surplus by purchasers of G/098-114 dated Sept 1918 (field Coy RE) returned to Base. 153 Periscopes Nos 9, returned Base mss GRO 5960.	GF.
—	23-1-19		Major J.J. Potter, ITC proceeded on three weeks leave to UK. 48th Sanitary Section transferred to me by OC 4th Corps Troops for General Stores. 59th Sanitary Section moved to Rabot 4th Division	GF
—	25-1-19		Wanted A.297 Youth Corps. with reference to stores being returned by Demobilised Units	GF

Army Form C. 2118.

WAR DIARY

INTELLIGENCE SUMMARY Sheet 3

(Erase heading not required.)

Instructions regarding War Diaries and Intelligence Summaries are contained in F. S. Regs., Part II. and the Staff Manual respectively. Title pages will be prepared in manuscript.

Place	Date	Hour	Summary of Events and Information	Remarks and references to Appendices
Chaulnes	28-1-19		Visited 22 & 45 OMW (Lights) with articles for repair.	S.W.
—	30-1-19		Visited Town Major with B.M. 39th Division, with reference to area required for "parking" vehicles should necessity arise.	S.W.

Tag	Krankengeschichte	Be-köstigung

SECRET

War Diary for month of February, 1919.

D.A.D.O.S. 42nd Divn.

Army Form C. 2118.

WAR DIARY
INTELLIGENCE SUMMARY.
(Erase heading not required.)

February 1919

Instructions regarding War Diaries and Intelligence Summaries are contained in F. S. Regs., Part II. and the Staff Manual respectively. Title pages will be prepared in manuscript.

Place	Date	Hour	Summary of Events and Information	Remarks and references to Appendices
Charleroi Belgium	1/2/19		Normal duty routine	
	2/2/19		do.	
	3/2/19		do.	
	4/2/19		do.	
	5/2/19		do.	
	6/2/19		do.	FS
	7/2/19		do.	
	8/2/19		do.	
	9/2/19		do.	
	10/2/19		do.	
	11/2/19		Units of the Division numbered to return to British Royales, Brussels, Ambrines & watches in accordance with Demobn. Regs. Caps X & XIX	FS
	12/2/19 to 19/2/19		Above mentioned articles received from units stored at 3 Rue du Rivage, Charleroi	FS
	20/2/19		Capt G. Hardy R.A.O.C & Cpl Bell R.A.O.C. left detachment for demobilisation	FS
	21/2/19			FS
	22/2/19		To be a/c. stores despatched to Achiet by trip y/c of L/Cpl Chetwood	FS
	23/2/19		Normal duty routine	FS
	28/2/19			FS

J. I. Potter Major
D.A.D.O.S. 42nd Division

www.ingramcontent.com/pod-product-compliance
Lightning Source LLC
Chambersburg PA
CBHW081551160426
43191CB00011B/1894